Educating
Women

Educating Women

Cultural Conflict and Victorian Literature

Laura Morgan Green

Ohio University Press

Athens

Ohio University Press, Athens, Ohio 45701
© 2001 by Laura Morgan Green
Printed in the United States of America

Ohio University Press books are printed on acid-free paper ∞™

09 08 07 06 05 04 03 02 01   5 4 3 2 1

Chapter 4 appeared previously in slightly different form in *Nineteenth Century Studies* 9 (1995): 1–30. Chapter 5 appeared previously in slightly different form in *Victorian Studies* 38 (1995): 523–49, published by Indiana University Press.

Library of Congress Cataloging-in-Publication Data

Green, Laura Morgan.
    Educating women: cultural conflict and Victorian literature
/ Laura Morgan Green.
        p. cm.
    Includes bibliographical references and index.
    ISBN 0-8214-1402-X – ISBN 0-8214-1403-8 (pbk.)
        1. English prose literature—19th century—History and criticism.
2. Women—Education (Higher)—Great Britain—History—19th
century. 3. Feminism and literature—Great Britain—History—
19th century. 4. Women and literature—Great Britain—History—
19th century. 5. English fiction—19th century—History and
criticism. 6. Feminist fiction, English—History and criticism. 7.
Women intellectuals—Great Britain—Biography. 8. Women
intellectuals in literature. 9. Education in literature. 10. Heroines in
literature. 11. Women in literature. I. Title.

PR 788.W6G74 2001
823'.809352042—dc21   2001036060

Contents

Acknowledgments

My thinking about women and education has evolved over the course of my own progress through educational institutions. My first thanks go to Mary Poovey for two seminars at Swarthmore College that revealed to me the transformative possibilities of feminist literary criticism. I pursued those possibilities to the English department of the University of California at Berkeley, where the book began as a dissertation, and I thank Catherine Gallagher, Carol Christ, and Thomas Laqueur for their guidance and their support then and since. Members of the Victorianist dissertation group, including Laura Berry, Michael Galchinsky, Daniel Hack, Kate McCullough, Catherine Robson, and Judith Rosen, offered helpful responses to various drafts, and Caren Kaplan encouraged my work on Anna Leonowens. I thank the Berkeley department of English and the Mabelle McLeod Lewis foundation for dissertation fellowships, and the regents of the university for a grant for travel to the Fawcett Library in London. At Yale University, an A. Whitney Griswold faculty grant enabled me to visit Westfield College, University of London, where Anselm Nye and Nick Holloway graciously provided access to the Constance Maynard archive. I am also grateful for the enthusiasm and efficiency of my editors at the Ohio

University Press and for the comments on the manuscript of two anonymous readers.

My pleasurable debt to Elizabeth Young and William Cohen, constant friends and ideal interlocutors, encompasses not only their readings of multiple drafts but also their championship at every stage of this project: the book is unimaginable without them. For intellectual engagement, professional support, and friendship in many combinations, I also thank: Linda Anderson, Mary Pat Brady, Julie Croston, Wai-Chee Dimock, Laurie Essig, Anne Flammang, Harriet Fraad, Jane Garrity, Kelly Hager, Kira Hall, Margaret Homans, Karen Jacobs, Carla Kaplan, Susan Lehman, Kate McCullough, Linda Peterson, William Rando, Steven Shareshian, Jackie Stevens, Michael Trask, Saskia van Dijl, Kerry Walk, Lisa Wedeen, Laura Wexler, Ara Wilson, Kate Wilson, and Denise Witzig. Debra Minkoff's example of professional and scholarly commitment has guided and sustained me. I have not forgotten the many forms of generosity of Martha Garcia. To my family, Philip, Dorothy, and Robert Green, I am variously grateful. My father's respectful and enthusiastic teaching of undergraduate women for over thirty years; my mother's knowledge of women's history and work for organizations supporting women today; and my brother's healthy skepticism toward institutions have shaped not only this book but also my intellectual life.

Introduction

The subject of this book is the relationship between two phenomena central to English culture in the second half of the nineteenth century—the movement to establish higher education for women, and the profusion of representations of women as students, teachers, or frustrated scholars within the domestic novel of the period. The women's education movement intersected with larger Victorian cultural conflicts over gender and identity, in particular a conflict between the values of domestic ideology and those of an emergent liberal individualism, provoking complex and often ambivalent responses even among its supporters. I analyze both fiction and nonfiction texts that revolve around themes of pedagogy and delineate a range of such responses, beginning with writings by educational reformers and including three novels—Charlotte Brontë's *Jane Eyre* (1847), George Eliot's *Middlemarch* (1872), and Thomas Hardy's *Jude the Obscure* (1896), and one memoir—Anna Leonowens's *The English Governess at the Siamese Court* (1870).

These four texts span a period of radical change in the relationship of middle-class English women to the educational institutions that served as the gateway to scholarly or professional authority. In 1847, when *Jane Eyre,* Brontë's first novel, appeared, no university in England was open to women. By 1896, when *Jude the Obscure,* Hardy's last novel, appeared, women were studying at Oxford and Cambridge and could receive degrees at universities throughout Great Britain. Beginning in the 1840s, as these changes occurred, women's intellectual ambitions increasingly became the subject of fictional narrative. In addition to the novels on which I focus, fictional representations include Tennyson's "medley," *The Princess* (1847), in which Tennyson fantasizes the founding and destruction of a women's college; Elizabeth Barrett Browning's novel-in-verse, *Aurora Leigh* (1857), a woman's *kunstlerroman* that begins with an indictment of the dilettante education conventionally given to middle-class women; Charlotte M. Yonge's *The Daisy Chain* (1856) and *The Clever Woman of the Family* (1865), in both of which the heroines court tragedy by pursuing intellectual ambitions at the expense of domestic duties; George Gissing's *The Odd Women* (1893), in which the protagonist runs a school of industry for young women; and George Bernard Shaw's play, *Mrs. Warren's Profession* (1898), whose "New Woman" heroine, Vivie Warren, has just left Cambridge with honors in mathematics.

On the one hand, it is not surprising that the effects of the higher education movement are legible in the domestic novel: it would be surprising if they were not. As Daniel Cottom argues, intellectuals of the English middle class in the nineteenth century "took their mission to be the creation of education as the matrix of social continuity" (33), and the novel became a privileged form for the dissemination of that ideal (35). Certainly women writers belonged to the cultural consensus on the desirability of spreading middle-class epistemologies that Cottom posits. On the other hand, the dominant ideal of education was based on middle-class *men's* experience, from which women's, whatever their class, diverged radically: for most of the century, their educability remained a question, not a fact, and they were not routinely included in large-scale plans of educational reform. Although writing and teaching, both of which required some degree of education, were among the few careers even grudgingly open to women at the beginning of the Victorian era, women's relationship to education was largely one of exclusion and drudgery. All the authors I discuss had experienced and been affected by these conditions. Eliot, whose own erudition, after a conventional education interrupted by her father's illness, was largely self-created, gave advice and funds for the foundation of Girton, the first Cambridge women's college. Brontë and Leonowens, both under financial strain, turned to authorship in part as an alternative to the underpaid and unregulated teaching careers open to women. Hardy began as an aspiring author whose lower-middle-class origins excluded him (as gender had excluded his schoolmistress sisters) from the educational resources of the intellectual elite.

This particular relationship to educational debates and institutions—a relationship of exclusion and contest—begins to account for the apparent indistinctness with which the topic actually appears in these authors' works: everywhere present as theme, rarely developed as incident. Backdating (as in *Middlemarch* and *Jane Eyre*), settings abroad (as in Leonowens's *English Governess at the Siamese Court*), and a focus on provincial characters and milieus (as in *Jude the Obscure*) place these texts at an apparent remove from the public debate and developments surrounding their creators. Although their protagonists are marked by their precarious status as potential or actual students or teachers, they struggle, die, or dwindle into domesticity in isolation from the organized movement for the higher education of women.

Instead, even as women's intellectual ambitions assumed importance in such narratives, and in the authors' own lives, novelists continued to thread those ambitions through the needle's eye of a plot of courtship and marriage that, if it bent under their weight, nevertheless refused to break. The conventions of this plot, which dominates the domestic novel of the eighteenth and nineteenth centuries, are familiar. Its protagonist is a middle-class woman; her milieu is the home; although she might begin her narrative trajectory with aspirations toward intellectual, artistic, or philanthropic achievement that distinguish her from her immediate peers—think of Elizabeth Bennet or Dorothea Brooke—her aspirations will ultimately be resolved in an appropriate marriage. The steps leading to and enabling this resolution—the heroine's tempering (in the case, for example, of Austen) or renunciation (in the case of Eliot or Yonge) of her desires—constitute the heroine's education.

Recently, feminist critics have stressed that the apparent stringencies of the marriage plot do not preclude, and perhaps enable, expressions of women's desires of various kinds. Unlike debates over education, for example, the domestic novel included and validated women's experience. As Ruth Bernard Yeazell writes, "A conventional courtship plot, even an insistent love story, undoubtedly subjected its heroine to narrow constraints. . . . [Nevertheless,] if the assumption of her modesty enabled the novelists to make her the subjective center of their narratives, to represent her as a subject was also to represent, however obliquely, her energies and desires" (237). Nancy Armstrong makes an even stronger claim, that the domestic novel actually arrogated a degree of power to women as agents and subjects of fictional representation: "Although concerned mainly with the vicissitudes of courtship and marriage, and fictional courtships and marriages at that, fiction that represented gender from this gendered viewpoint exerted a form of political authority" (30).

At the same time, however, if the domestic novel included women's experience by attending to their roles within domestic ideology, it also propagated those roles by its continued cultural reproduction, and frequent valorization, of them. Furthermore, the domestic novel remains structured by a series of antinomies between female and male experience, private and public space, personal and political relations. These antinomies both require and justify the mediating closure of marriage. Within this structure, there was little room for the alternative narrative that was emerging from the women's higher education movement, for this narrative tended to blur these oppositions. This account of female intellectual ambition would have a corporate, rather than an individual, protagonist; would take place partly in public and institutional settings (i.e., colleges) that nevertheless stressed the private and internal occupations of study and contemplation; and would trace the movement of that protagonist not from maidenhood to marriage and the conventional closure of social reproduction but from the tragic position of downtrodden governesses to the open-ended status of university scholar.

The problem with this alternative was not that it was, in any literal way, opposed to the teleology of marriage—reformers protested such an imputation strenuously at every opportunity. The problem was rather that, whatever the protestations of the reformers, the extension of higher education to women, and their incursion into public spaces and competitive relations previously reserved for men, dislodged women from their narrative status as a special kind of subject, a private subject, with a special kind of story—a story about domestic relations. At the same time, because the ideology and rhetoric of the higher education movement remained profoundly indebted to the same conceptions of the social meaning of gender that underwrote the marriage plot, and because of the youth and uncertainty of the movement itself, it did not offer a completely realized or realizable counternarrative.

The context of the debate over women's education, therefore, does not alter the domestic novel's antinomic structure and the teleology of the marriage plot. Rather, the novel assimilates the terms of the debate to its own narrative exigencies, in the form of a variety of conflicts between the intellectual ambitions of the female protagonist and the social demands she encounters. Each of the texts I discuss illuminates a particular iteration of this contest. The first chapter, on the rhetoric of the movement, examines the ways in which the writings of activists both resist and recuperate the role played by women within the narrative of domestic ideology. In the second chapter, the conflict is between the emergent, self-directed values of liberal individualism and the declining, other-directed values of domestic ideology in *Jane Eyre;* in the third, between a model of feminine influence and an aspiration toward female scholarly and pedagogical authority in Anna Leonowens's fictionalized memoir, *The English Governess at the Siamese Court;* in the fourth, between an ideal of intellection as private, internal, and essentially amateur, associated with women, and a counterideal, questioned in George Eliot's *Middlemarch,* of knowledge as public, professional, and institutional, associated with men; and finally, in the fifth chapter, between a Victorian understanding of masculine and feminine intellect as essentially opposed mental forces, housed in fully differentiated anatomies, and a modern understanding of intellect as to some degree androgynous, an opposition staged in *Jude the Obscure.*

Educating Women, then, itself aims to undermine an opposition— between the apparent progressivism of a historical narrative of educating women, and the apparent conservatism of a fictional structure of marrying them off.

Educating
Women

Chapter 1

Domesticity and Duplicity
The Rhetoric of the Higher Education Movement

In 1868, Emily Davies (1830–1921), the leader of the movement for the higher education of women, was struggling to raise money and support for the foundation of what would become Girton College, Cambridge, the first institution in Britain to offer women the same education that male undergraduates received.[1] Counseling patience in the face of opposition, she wrote to a colleague:

> I often think of St. Paul, with his sensitive, highly strung, nervous temperament, and the amount of worry he went thro', with the care of all the churches upon him, all quarrelling and fretting and disgracing themselves, and he, *feeling* it all to the heart's core, held on, appealing and persuading and remonstrating, and every now and then coming out with songs of triumph. It makes one's own vexations look small. (Qtd. in Stephen, 169–70; emphasis in the original.)

To the feminist reader, on the one hand, the analogy may seem inapposite. Paul was no supporter of women's intellectual emancipation: "Let the women keep silence in the churches," he famously enjoined, "for it is not permitted unto them to speak; but let them be in subjection, as also saith the law. And if they would learn anything, let them ask their own husbands at home, for it is shameful for a woman to speak in church" (1 Cor. 14:34). To the doctrinally conservative reader, on the other hand, the analogy might seem overreaching, if not blasphemous, since Davies implicitly equates the importance of the foundation of higher education for women with that of the establishment of Christianity, not so much making her "vexations look small," as she claims, as writing them large. Like so many of Davies's utterances, then, this one has an ambiguous ideological valence—apparently orthodox in its vocabulary, potentially radical in its implications.

Inasmuch as learning, in Paul's time, was substantially ecclesiastical, his adjuration confides a woman's entire intellectual development to her husband's guardianship. In the second half of the nineteenth century, women's religious authority had grown greatly within the home, but they were still expected to "keep silence" not only within the church but in all public spaces. From most public institutions, including institutions of higher education, they were debarred. Paul's injunction continued to provide authority for the prohibition against women's public presence and speech.[2] Not surprisingly, given this tradition, some women in the higher education movement were uncomfortable with the public speaking and advocacy it required—Davies, for example, on several occasions in the 1860s and 1870s asked male supporters to read her papers on women's education for her at meetings of the liberal National Association for the Promotion of Social Science (NAPSS) (Stephen, 94 n. 1; Caine, *Victorian Feminists,* 99–100). Yet the cause for which they were working—to bring women's education out of the home and into public institutions, to provide women with direct access to learning and the training to diffuse it—took direct and inevitable aim at the Pauline injunction and the gendered division of knowledge and labor it supported. When she invokes Paul, Davies speaks with a forked tongue. Her letter exemplifies the doubled and paradoxical relations between the logic and effect of the higher education movement, which fundamentally challenged the organization of Victorian society and family into separate spheres of activity for men and women that we now call "domestic ideology," and the ideological roots and rhetoric of its leaders, who had been formed by domestic ideology, and often by the Evangelical religious tradition associated with it, remained attached to many of the values it instated, and perceived their own activism as indebted to those values even as it challenged many of their effects.[3] Davies's letter demonstrates some of these attachments and some of the rhetorical strategies by which the activists negotiated between tradition and innovation.

Davies's familiarity with Scripture, as a clergyman's daughter and a Church of England adherent all her life, is not surprising, but her evocation of Paul goes beyond familiarity to declare a sympathetic intimacy and even identification with her subject.[4] Her words insistently feminize and domesticate Paul. The church leaders, "quarrelling and fretting and disgracing themselves," sound like nothing so much as a large family, and the "sensitive" apostle, with his heartfelt *"feeling"* and his womanly methods of proselytizing—"appealing and persuading and remonstrating"— sounds very like the moral matron of the domestic ideal. Displaying her knowledge of Scripture, Davies asserts her loyalty to the distinctly patriarchal religious and familial structures of her own upbringing, which was defined by her father's combative Evangelicalism (Caine, *Victorian Feminists*, 61) and the conventions of her own role as a clergyman's daughter, which she described in a letter as "twenty years at Gateshead . . . *all* schools and District visiting" (qtd. in Stephen, 123). At the same time, her analogy redefines the meaning of that loyalty by portraying her as the speaking colleague rather than the silenced dependent of masculine authority. If Paul is represented as a woman, Davies is represented as Paul, like him a proselyte and writer of hortatory epistles. In this way, she rhetorically and imaginatively mediates a conflict between the Pauline prohibition on women's independent intellectual ambition and the destabilizing implications of her own project. Reappropriating rather than rejecting the Evangelical tradition, she can assert in *The Higher Education of Women* (1866) that "the theory of education of our English Church recognizes no distinction of sex" (15). Her analogy of herself with Saint Paul produces the lack of distinction that she claims to discover as authorization for her project.[5]

The subject of this chapter is the way in which, as in Davies's letter, the rhetoric of the higher education movement drew on, grappled with, and reappropriated the domestic ideological tradition that assigned to women responsibility for the maintenance and superintendence of the home, the family, and the private virtues of religion and morality. The rhetorical record of the movement takes both private forms (letters, diaries, unpublished memoirs) and public ones (books, pamphlets, and speeches). It is by no means unified, either across these forms or among the women who participated in the movement. These women were almost uniformly middle class and upper-middle class, but their political and religious backgrounds varied, from the middle-class Davies, Church of England in religion and Conservative in politics, to Josephine Butler (1828–1906), who came from a background in the landed gentry and whose activism was motivated by deep Evangelical faith and Liberal political connections. As the schoolmistress and activist Elizabeth Wolstenholme noted, the higher education movement was "conceived in the interests of women by women themselves" (Wolstenholme-Elmy, 147), regardless of their internal divisions and distinctions. Those divisions, however, meant that the movement neither grew from nor developed a single liberationist ideology but rather worked to adapt prevailing ideologies of gender and also of class to the changing needs, financial and social, of middle-and upper-middle-class women in the latter half of the nineteenth century.[6]

The higher education movement, which began modestly in the 1840s with the foundation of two schools for improving the instruction of governesses, laid the foundation for a half-century of political action that culminated in women's achievement of the suffrage.[7] In 1837, when Queen Victoria came to the throne, no institution of higher education in Great Britain was open to women. By the end of the century, they could matriculate at Oxford, Cambridge, the University of London, Durham University, all of the newly chartered civic universities, and universities in Scotland, Ireland, and Wales. Histories of the movement for women's higher education have detailed the legislative and institutional developments that enabled this rapid alteration, such as the founding of Queen's (1848) and Bedford (1849) Colleges; the inclusion of girls' schools in the purview of the Taunton (Schools' Inquiry) Commission that investigated middle-class secondary education in England (1864–68); the opening of Girton College, Cambridge (as Hitchin College in 1869); the passing of the Endowed Schools Act (1869), which opened up funds for girls' education; the opening of all degrees of the University of London to women (1878); and the founding of various Oxford and Cambridge women's colleges from the 1870s on. Given the movement's emphasis on intellectual and moral equality and access to the public sphere, it appears to exemplify the liberal individualist roots of "first wave" feminism, and its trajectory can appear revolutionary in both the speed and the nature of the changes it brought about.

This impression of rapid and significant change is simultaneously misleading and suggestive. Materially speaking, it is misleading: access to higher education directly altered the lives of a very small minority of women in England in the nineteenth century. Numbers of women undergraduates grew slowly during the period; by 1900, according to Carol Dyhouse, women made up only 16 percent of students in institutions of higher education in Great Britain (17). Given the small number of people, female or male, attending universities at all in the nineteenth and first half of the twentieth century in England—only 1 percent of the age bracket, according to Gillian Sutherland, as late as 1914 (157)—this proportion represents a very small absolute number of female students, largely drawn from a homogeneous social stratum of the professional and the leisured classes (Dyhouse, 23–24).

Women were not only a numerical minority of students; they were also marginalized by the universities even as they were admitted to them. Women involved in university education in the 1870s and early 1880s often did not take the same classes or exams as men, receive the same or indeed any degrees upon completion of their course of study, or have the same rights of institutional affiliation. By the late 1880s and 1890s, B.A. degrees for women on the same terms as men were common at the newer universities in England and universities in Scotland and Wales (Dyhouse, 12). The ancient English foundations held out, however: at Oxford, women were not admitted to the B.A. degree until 1919, at Cambridge, not until 1948. Exclusion from degrees disqualified women from institutional governance and affected the availability of scholarship support, which in any case lagged behind that of male students (Dyhouse, 27–31). If women students went on to become scholars, they experienced prohibitive discrimination in funding, teaching opportunities, and institutional affiliation. Their lack of a recognized credential upon graduation could also be a barrier in other professions.[8]

If the material effects of the higher education movement were limited and uneven, the same is true of its direct ideological impact. As the historian Barbara Caine points out, "The assumption that feminism was an offshoot of liberalism has . . . been questioned in the light of a growing interest in the religious, the socialist, and even the conservative roots of feminism on the one hand, and an increasing awareness of the very problematical relationship between feminism and liberalism on the other" (*Victorian Feminists,* 3). As Caine argues, Victorian domestic ideology was not only the opponent of, but also a formative influence on, Victorian feminism, precisely to the extent that the moral and religious responsibilities it attributed to women could be called upon to justify philanthropy and social action as responses to the "needs . . . of the wider society." But that extent was always limited and contested (85). As one of the more prolific propagandists of the domestic ideal, Sarah Stickney Ellis, asserted, "Much as may be said, and said justly, in praise of the public virtues of women, . . . could the question of superiority on these two points be universally proposed, a response would be heard throughout the world, in favour of woman in her private and domestic character" (49). Feminists—the higher education activists among them—who called upon the rhetoric of the domestic ideal to justify their occupation of public and institutional space were never simply citing but always emending it, pushing domestic ideology to its limits even as that ideology in turn limited the scope and nature of their claims.

Women associated with higher education certainly transgressed ordinary social expectations. Commenting on "Female Education" in 1869, a writer for the *Quarterly Review* firmly summarizes these expectations and their implications for women's education: "The sphere of women is home. Such a cultivation as will make a really good wife, sister, or daughter, to educated men, is the thing to be aimed at. . . . There will always be something inconsistent with the idea of a fit channel for receiving such true cultivation in a system where adult women are lectured by men . . . where strictly intellectual pursuits are exclusively pursued *away from home*" (465–66; emphasis added). Because of these expectations, most of the first students enrolled at Girton had to conquer not only strong familial objections but also their own feelings of transgression. Davies commented that she was "more and more impressed with the difficulties of conscience in the way of young women, as I hear more about them. They think they ought not to urge their own wishes against those of their parents" (qtd. in Stephen, 211). Anna Lloyd enjoyed only four terms at the college before bowing to pressure to withdraw from her family, for whom her studies were a pursuit "merely of self-indulgence and self-satisfaction, distracting her from the plain duties that lay before her" (qtd. in Bradbrook, 4). Constance Maynard, later principal of Evangelical Westfield College, was permitted to enroll only after promising that she would stay for only a year and not pursue a degree, a limitation that was later withdrawn (Stephen, 212). The "self-indulgence" involved in pursuing independent study was seen as a transgression against religious, as well as filial, principle. One oft-quoted anecdote has a clergyman condemning Hitchin, the forerunner of Girton, as "that *infidel* place" (qtd. in Bradbrook, 3), although Emily Davies had insisted that the college offer Church of England services and instruction in order to avoid precisely such criticism (Stephen, 263–66). Again, these anxieties were internal as well as externally imposed. Maynard, coming from an almost fantastically sheltered Evangelical background, was deeply distressed by the lack of emphasis on religion at Girton (Vicinus, *Independent Women,* 157).

Participation in the movement, therefore, required a degree of strong-mindedness in the face of opposition. But it did not necessarily indicate or foster other kinds of politically progressive, radical, or even egalitarian beliefs or behavior. The middle-and upper-middle-class women who pursued university-level study had no thought of losing their claim to gentility. The aim was not to overthrow the dominion of "respectability," nor even to challenge the powerful determination of gender and class in setting its boundaries, but to extend them to include university study. The women's colleges could not avoid the definitive breach of decorum involved in "strictly intellectual pursuits . . . exclusively pursued *away from home,*" but they compensated by minimizing its impact, by turning spaces that were "away from home" into home-like spaces marked by their attention to propriety. Aside from Girton, which aimed from the first to achieve full equality with the men's colleges, the foundations for women that appeared in the 1870s at Cambridge and Oxford (Newnham at Cambridge and Lady Margaret and Somerville Halls at Oxford) were begun as residential halls for women pursuing nondegree studies (lecture series and study for the "Higher Local" examinations) and were guided by women whose social position more than outweighed their lack of academic credentials. Newnham College, for example, was presided over by Anne Clough (sister of the poet Arthur Hugh Clough), who "approached her duties as head of a women's college in more of the spirit of the schoolmistress than of a college don" (qtd. in Phillips, 1), and was so "terrified of the girls giving a bad impression in the Cambridge streets" that she admonished them not to button their gloves as they walked (Glendinning, 51). Women were chaperoned at lectures and curtailed in their access to mixed-sex spaces such as libraries and laboratories; their dress, speech, and deportment were monitored and corrected.[9] Davies interdicted ball playing on the lawn and theater performances at Girton and was shocked by the students' "spirit of revolt, and . . . self-confidence" (Stephen, 225, 243).

This concern with convention, which was both externally imposed and internally generated, is, however, not simply evidence of a class-determined social conservatism. It is also an example of the movement's double relationship to the rhetoric of domestic ideology. For the first generation of students, at least, these restrictions were partly a conscious performance that attempted to bury the assumptions underlying norms of female propriety even as it praised their visible expression. M. A. Quiggin, a member of the Newnham class of 1899, remembered

> The chief aim of the College was to be as inconspicuous as possible. Anything conspicuous in dress or behaviour was strongly disapproved . . . even on the hockey field we were expected to have skirts below the knee. One of our team had to write home for permission to leave off her flannel petticoat when playing hockey. . . . In my time one student got engaged while she was still up, and we were all rather disapproving. She was a research student and got engaged to the lecturer who was coaching her. We felt it was a breach of academic propriety. (Phillips, 45–46)

While the first part of the passage vacillates among representing "propriety" as a corporate endeavor ("The chief aim of the College was to be as inconspicuous as possible") and something externally imposed ("we were expected to have skirts below the knee"), in both cases it assumes conventional expectations of feminine behavior that suspected any corporeal display in unmarried women. The second part, however, reformulates propriety in ways that undermine those expectations. Marriage itself—the conventional goal of domestic ideology—becomes the "breach" of propriety, and the relevant standard becomes academic, rather than sexual. In a similar reminiscence, Maynard remembers the same kind of self-censorship, with the same goal: "The main idea in all these matters was to escape observation." She adds, "It may seem but a poor object for which to work, that we might win the commendation given by that exclusively feminine word 'nice,' but it was the best of all shelters for our secretly growing and maturing cause" ("Autobiography," 183). Maynard's aside, even more explicitly than Quiggin's anecdote, formulates escaping "observation" as strategy rather than as simple conformity to the expectation that women would be invisible in public and institutional space. At the same time, however, it leaves open the question of when and under what circumstances that strategy will cease to be necessary or what alternative form of behavior will emerge when the "exclusively feminine word 'nice'" is finally deemed insufficient. Later generations of university women rebelled more openly against these restrictions.

The moment in 1868 at which Davies, "quivering with excitement, thinly veiled under a business-like manner" (qtd. in Stephen, 219) opened the door of a rented house in Hitchin to five young women, was the outcome of twenty years of debate over the purpose and appropriate form of the education of women. For most of the previous century, it had been taken for granted that an education consisting of decorative "accomplishments" was best suited to girls of the comfortable classes, and this education, such as it was, ended with marriage. At the turn of the century, Evangelically influenced educators such as Hannah More and Maria Edgeworth campaigned for a higher degree of moral seriousness in the preparation of girls for their duties as wives and mothers. By the middle of the nineteenth century, therefore, the position that women required no systematic intellectual training could not be seriously sustained.[10] But women's education was still conceived of as the training of girls, ideally within the home, to undertake with due seriousness their future roles as wives and mothers. The principles of such training were elaborated in a new literature of "household education" that inherited many of its assumptions from the conduct literature of the late eighteenth century, taking a homiletic tone and emphasizing moral development and responsibilities.[11]

The books published in rapid succession throughout the 1840s by the prolific and popular Sarah Stickney Ellis are representative of this genre, its rhetoric, and its assumptions. The volumes' very titles, with their repetition of the words "domestic," "influence," and "duties" and its synonyms ("obligations," "responsibilities") and their entire avoidance of words such as "education" or "learning," summarize the prevailing concerns. *The Women of England, Their Social Duties, and Domestic Habits* (1839), *The Wives of England, Their Relative Duties, Domestic Influence, and Social Obligations* (1843), *The Mothers of England: Their Influence and Responsibility* (1843), and *The Daughters of England: Their Position in Society, Character, and Responsibilities* (1842) combined a celebration of middle-class domestic culture with fervent elaborations of the virtues of feminine submission, self-suppression, and devotion to domestic duty. "A high-minded and intellectual woman is never more truly great," Ellis writes, in *The Women of England*,

> than when willingly and judiciously performing kind offices
> for the sick; and much as may be said, and said justly, in
> praise of the public virtues of women . . . could the question
> of superiority on these two points be universally proposed, a
> response would be heard throughout the world, in favour of
> woman in her private and domestic character. (49)

Ellis's rhetoric, however, has its own moments of tension, if not actual doubleness. She does not deny the existence of "a high-minded and intellectual woman." She expects and advocates the voluntary suppression that will bring such a woman into greater conformity with the demands of the feminine role as she understands it, and she understands that such suppression is not natural but learned: "I still cling fondly to the hope, that, ere long, some system of female instruction will be discovered, by which the young women of England may be sent home from school prepared for the stations appointed them by Providence to fill in after life" (103). But her exposition offers no explanation of the paradox whereby Providence should appoint a woman to a "station" that can be filled only by "lay[ing] aside . . . her very *self*—and assuming a new nature" (52).

By the end of the 1840s, however, a different critique of girls' education had begun to emerge, as its conception as a matter of strictly domestic and moral training began to appear inadequate. Because the aim of such training was the reproduction and recirculation of domestic virtues, it presupposed and depended upon the continued absorption of women in the domestic sphere. The growing visibility of single, self-supporting middle-class women—variously attributed to the economic depression of the 1840s, which left fathers of large families unable to provide for their daughters; the tendency of young men of business to delay marriage; and the "surplus" of women over men in the population, revealed in the census of 1851—brought this ideal narrative up against a more vicious circle. Middle-class women who needed to support themselves conventionally became governesses, a position that in principle allowed them to earn a living while maintaining their appropriate role as reproducers of the domestic ideal. But as products themselves of that ideal, they frequently found themselves able to do neither: they "cannot teach, because they are so ill educated, and again, they are so ill educated that they can do nothing *but* teach" (Butler, "Education and Employment of Women," 79), and the oversupply of poorly qualified governesses lowered both the prestige and the wages of the profession.

Immediate responses to the breakdown in the domestic ideal represented by the plight of the governess attempted to contain the problems she represented by treating her as a tragic exception, rather than a challenge, to contemporary class and gender arrangements.[12] The Governesses' Benevolent Institution (founded 1841; reorganized 1843) began by providing charitable annuities to retired governesses whose low wages had not allowed them to save enough money to live on, but the founders soon recognized that improved standards would be necessary to raise the actual wages they received. Out of this realization grew Queen's College (1848) and Bedford College (1849), whose original aim was to provide training and credentials for women in the teaching profession. As Martha Vicinus points out, their founders were not motivated by a conception of women's higher education as an end in itself. "Both [Bedford and Queen's] colleges were almost wholly nonresidential and placed much emphasis upon making up deficiencies in their students' education. . . . [N]otions of providing a separate environment for women, in which full-time study and independence from family duties would be key elements, were rejected" (123). The effect of these institutions, however, exceeded and reshaped their original ideological impetus. By producing a small group of women who began to reform and reorganize girls' secondary schools, which in turn produced graduates who themselves were prepared and eager to engage in systematic teaching or study, they created a self-perpetuating constituency for the reform of women's education.[13]

In the 1850s, such women began to produce books on women's education that altered the discourse of the preceding generation's domestic homilies in a number of ways. Continuing to assume that women were centered in the home and that their most important learning and teaching occurred there, they nevertheless devoted attention to intellectual development rather than simply moral conduct. Maria Shirreff (later Grey) and Emily Shirreff, both active in girls' education, addressed themselves to leisured women like themselves in their *Thoughts on Self-Culture, Addressed to Women* (1850) and in Emily Shirreff's *Intellectual Education, and Its Influence on the Character and Happiness of Women* (1858). Like Ellis's, the titles are themselves revealing. Where for Ellis the self was the enemy to be repressed—she went so for as to chastise schools for emphasizing "improvement of *self*, so far as relates to intellectual attainments" (74)—the Shirreffs emphasize the good of "*self-culture*" (emphasis added), which is "the cultivation of the intellect and the development of the reasoning faculties" (4). And in the later book, "happiness" has joined "character" as an important outcome of women's education, replacing Ellis's emphasis on "duties" and "obligation."

Despite these indications that they conceive of women as intellectually autonomous and capable of gaining personal pleasure from intellection, the Shirreffs' arguments and vocabulary remain indebted to the assumptions of domestic ideology. Like Ellis, Emily Shirreff in *Intellectual Education and Its Influence on the Character and Happiness of Women* assumes that the middle- and upper-middle-class women whom she addresses will find their primary occupation within the home, as wives and mothers; and the text includes many references to the paticular demands of women's subordinate position. "As a question of happiness," she writes, "I believe devotion to one pursuit not to be desirable for women. They are not destined to 'achieve greatness,' and the means of doing so are seldom open to them, even had they the power" (80). Again, however, she demonstrates concern with women's "happiness" as individuals, although she does not explicitly protest against the lack of "means" that prevent them from what she clearly regards as the pleasures of "greatness." Her descriptions of the effects of "the natural and inevitable subordination of women" (295) can sound remarkably like protests, and they tend to highlight the negative aspects of domestic life: "In a life so exposed [as a woman's] to narrowing influences it is desirable to create as wide an interest as we can in all that is worthily exciting human thought and enterprise" (81).

Indeed, unlike Ellis, for whom women's domestic leisure and exemption from wage labor merely provide new opportunities for womanly self-sacrifice—"being the least engaged member of [the family], I am consequently the most at liberty to devote myself to the general good of the whole" (30)—Shirreff frankly regards housework both as drudgery and as an occupation that cannot engage any well-organized woman for very long. It is these conditions that, according to Shirreff, not only justify but necessitate the housewife's intellectual development:

> The very fact that women have no professions to exercise
> their abilities, or make them feel the need of knowledge,
> which has been the plea for giving them little or no solid
> mental cultivation, is then in truth, as I said above, the rea-
> son why they need a higher and more severe tone of educa-
> tion; since . . . they must be educated to feel from within
> what comes to the more active portion of mankind from
> without. (29)

Women's domestic "character" becomes the rationale for her intellectual education.

Shirreff never rejects the domestic ideal; in her conclusion, she explicitly rejects "the whole discussion of comparative claims, and powers, and rights [of women and men]" (424). Nevertheless, she turns the ideal's pedagogical theory on its head: the well-run household becomes the site of an engaged pedagogy for girls and women, and moral seriousness emerges not from self-denial but from contemplation of scientific discoveries: "astronomy, which . . . first kindled in man the spirit of inquiry into the order of nature" and "the beauty of chemical laws and phenomena, carrying the mind in contemplation from the minutest and commonest things to powers that are almost sublime in their reach and magnitude" (59). And despite her scorn for a "dream of [sexual] equality

. . . born of wild political theory," Shirreff herself asserts the credo of moral and intellectual equality that will become one of the basic tenets of the higher education movement: "Education . . . has one and the same purpose for every human being; and this purpose is the systematic and harmonious development of his whole moral and intellectual nature. It follows that the elementary principles must be the same for all" (7). Shirreff's simultaneous commitment to a domestic role for women and the "development of [the] whole moral and intellectual nature" for "every human being" causes her some difficulties. Viewing the domestic world women must inhabit as essentially confining, but unwilling to question the necessity of that confinement, she seeks to enlarge it through "cultivation." Yet this same cultivation may make women unhappy by reminding them of their exclusion from opportunities for "greatness"—and perhaps, although she does not explicitly say so, lead to "wild political theor[ies]." (She does touch on hysteria and depression as psychological problems to which women's confined lives make them particularly prone.)

The same period saw the emergence of a discourse more directly in opposition to domestic ideology, which asserted the necessity for many women to be self-supporting and linked the agitation for improved education directly to that need. This priority is clearly legible in the approximately forty articles, letters, and reviews on the subject of women's education published over the six-year life span (1858–64) of the *English Woman's Journal*—the first periodical in England directed to middle-class women to focus on public rather than domestic affairs.[14] The journal (which Davies briefly edited) was run out of offices in Langham Place that served as headquarters for the London women's movement and housed, among other organizations and activities, the Society for the Promotion of Employment for Women (SPEW, founded in 1859) and the Female Middle Class Emigration Society, both of which directly addressed the problems of single, working women of the middle classes. Its audience—never large—was both other activists and middle-class working women. In this context, education was conceived of largely as a means to the end of providing middle-class women with respectable work, and making work respectable; the *English Woman's Journal* writers had little patience with those—like Shirreff—who did not give primacy to this link. A review of *Intellectual Education* in the journal complains that

Miss Shirreff regards the general adoption of professional life by women as an impossibility. . . but neither, on the other hand, does she favor the idea of "well-to-do" women taking an active part in household concerns. Here we think is her great and abiding mistake. She does not value action as the only medium in which any human creature can become either good or great. Far rather would we see our little maidens baking and brewing, cutting and darning, rather than spending all their time in "cultivating their minds" without any definite ulterior aim. (345)

In her revolt against cultivation, the reviewer (probably the editor, Bessie Rayner Parkes) comes close to subordinating education altogether to "action"; she also neatly elides the distinction that Shirreff preserves between feminine "goodness" and masculine "greatness." This position can be simply pragmatic, as in Butler's assertion, ten years later, that "[t]he simultaneousness of the demand for industrial freedom and for higher education is based on a necessity. The education which most women need is one which will fit them for business in professions or in industries" (qtd. in Levine, 129). Here, however, the writer's assertion is also idealist and polemical. Valuing "action" as a "medium" for women, even rhetorically, is in itself an activist step, since Shirreff's cultivated lady and Ellis's self-sacrificing matron continued more accurately to embody the cultural consensus on women's role.

In the mid-1860s, then, when Davies began talking with supportive Cambridge dons about the possibility of opening a college for women there, the reformist view of women's educational needs encompassed two somewhat different emphases—on "cultivation" and on "action." Davies admired cultivation because she admired upper-class manners and decorous behavior; she always sought women with these qualities to fill the role of mistress at Girton. When Emily Shirreff, some years later, agreed to take this position for two terms, Davies wrote to a colleague that Shirreff had "a stoical way of talking which attracts me. . . . She is I believe about 55, ladylike and gentle in manner, and I fancy a good deal of a student" and "moves in such high circles that scarcely anybody I know has ever seen her" (qtd. in Stephen, 227–28). But the medium in which Davies herself flourished, and out of which Girton was built, was action. "The case of the modern girl is peculiarly hard in this," she wrote in *Higher Education,* "that she has fallen upon an age in which idleness is accounted disgraceful. . . . Everywhere we hear that true happiness is to be found in work" (44). Davies in many ways exemplified that "modern girl" with her devotion to "work." But the "age in which idleness is accounted disgraceful" was defined for Davies and her cohort as much by an old-fashioned, Evangelically influenced emphasis on labor and duty and rejection of frivolity as by a modern, liberal notion of self-development. (As Caine comments, "Davies's Evangelical background made it impossible for her to experience pleasure in social life without guilt" [*Victorian Feminists,* 71]). Davies first became involved in the problem of women's education in the 1850s, when, on occasional visits to her clergyman brother in London, she began to organize support for the grueling, decade-long attempt of her friend Elizabeth Garrett (later Anderson) to qualify for a British medical degree. Throughout her activist career, as Janet Howarth writes, she "identified chiefly with the cause of the professional woman, the schoolmistress or aspiring doctor, who needed to demonstrate that her qualifications were not inferior to those of men" (xlv). In fact, Davies had no theory of pedagogy, only (although she would not likely have stated it this way) a theory of power: an accurate assessment of the importance of elite institutions such as Oxford and Cambridge in controlling access to professional life.

It was this understanding, rather than a commitment either to abstract equality or to the particular intellectual content of the Cambridge curriculum, that led her to insist that the standards, course and length of study, and examinations for the women students at Girton be the same as those of male undergraduates. "We are not fighting for the existing [examinations]. . . . What we are fighting for is the common standard for women and men without in the least committing ourselves to the opinion that the ultimate best has as yet been reached in any examination" (qtd. in Caine, *Victorian Feminists,* 89). Like the emphasis on "fighting," Davies's insistence on a "common standard" was controversial. It led her into conflict not only with more conservative opponents, who, like the dean of Canterbury, "deprecate[d] introducing anything like *competition* or personal public *designation* into the characteristic of female society in England" (qtd. in Caine, *Victorian Feminists,* 101), but also with other reformers. The Cambridge men involved, such as Henry Sidgwick and J. R. Seeley, were exasperated by her devotion to what they saw as an "old and . . . obsolete routine" (qtd. in Caine, *Victorian Feminists,* 88) of moribund classical and mathematical study, which they were trying to change. And women such as Ann Clough and Josephine Butler, who had been active in arranging alternative educational opportunities for women, such as the lecture series in Cambridge backed by Sidgwick, conceived them as an opportunity for mental cultivation and saw no reason to force sketchily educated women immediately to follow a course of study for which male undergraduates had had some ten years of preparation. The opposition of these groups—the clash between action and cultivation—provoked some of Davies's bitterest epistolary rhetoric. "I am sure it is generous inconsistency," she wrote to Henry Sidgwick, "and not cruel mockery that makes you say you are willing to help us, when your scheme is the serpent which is gnawing at our vitals" (qtd. in Stephen, 255).

Davies's opposition to "special systems" of women's education was expressed not only privately, in letters, but also publicly. The campaign for a college for women brought about a new kind of textual production with a new rhetoric and audience. Where previous books on domestic education had been directed at women in the home, Davies and Butler, along with other activists such as Barbara Bodichon and Frances Power Cobbe, began in the 1860s to write and edit lectures, pamphlets, and books directed to a larger public outside the home—to policy and opinion makers. These works, such as Emily Davies's *The Higher Education of Women,* which began as an address to the NAPSS, and "Special Systems of Education for Women" (1868), and Josephine Butler's essay, "The Education and Employment of Women" (1868), were directed to men who made policy. Davies's "Home and the Higher Education" (1878) which also addressed parents, addressed them not, as Ellis and Shirreff had, in their role as reproducers of the domestic ideal within the home, but in order to persuade them to educate their daughters *away* from home and to consider what role they might have in public life.

Davies and Butler shared a conviction that women and men were morally and intellectually equal and that this equality was founded in Christian theology. Davies, as we have already seen, asserted that "the Christian theory of education implies an essential resemblance between the sexes" (173); Butler, whose vocabulary was, without embarrassment, that of Christian witness, wrote that "It is in the name of *Christ* that the removal of burdens and disabilities is preached . . . this is the Person in whom all virtues which are considered essentially womanly, as well as those which are considered essentially manly, found their perfect development" (81). Both wrote polemical essays that depended partly on demonstrations of factual rigor, objectivity, and concrete application. Thus Butler's essay makes a display of empirical information: she begins by quoting figures from the 1861 census to demonstrate the numbers of "women who work for their own subsistence" (70), analyzes the salary range of Manchester governesses (71), and breaks the opposition to women's employment down into "three principal obstacles" (75) which she then discusses in order. Davies begins *Higher Education* by promising an objective "inquiry of a practical nature" (1). Although she does not cite facts and figures, she offers other forms of concrete evidence. She cites literary evidence by writers from Shakespeare to Coventry Patmore; she invites her audience to "bring before [the] mind's eye the picture of an English home" (94); and she concludes with "specific suggestions" for women's education. She also takes care to acknowledge and meet objections to her case: "It is true," she concedes, "that fathers are likely to hesitate in spending money on what may seem a doubtful speculation as regards pecuniary returns [i.e., the education of their daughters]" (100), but she then goes on to show why this investment would not be a "doubtful speculation."

Butler and Davies also both attempt to motivate their audiences with shame as well as reason, and it is here that the difference in their rhetorical styles becomes particularly evident. Butler's language is the more emotional, but she takes care to speak more in sorrow than in anger: "God knows it all, and if men do not know it, it is because they have been, I will not say they are, cruelly and criminally thoughtless. I wish some of those men who talk as if they imagined our life a delightful one, could but be women for one little year, and could feel the dreariness I speak of" (73). Davies, on the other hand, is frequently sarcastic, but her tone is always unemotional, and the object of her wit is never specified as "men": "It seems to be forgotten that women have always been married," she observes, while making the radical argument that women need not necessarily give up their professions on marriage. "Marriage is not a modern discovery, offering a hitherto untrodden field for feminine energy" (103). She also makes frequent use of the device of the rhetorical question and the invocation of common wisdom, which enable her to ridicule opposing arguments without appearing to attack a particular opponent: "'Women's work,' *it is said,* 'is helping work.' Certainly it is. And is it men's work to hinder?" (165; emphasis added). In the conclusion to *Higher Education,* she writes of the objection that women's emancipation will destroy the social safeguard of male chivalry: "The advocates of the protective theory seem scarcely to have realised that the idea of protection implies the corresponding idea of attack. It assumes, as part of its essence, that somebody is attacking, or what occasion would there be for defence? Might it not be well for *everybody* to abandon the attitude of attack?" (181–82). The refusal to attribute the conventional wisdom to any group in particular, as well as the use of rhetorical questions, enables Davies to minimize the often radical implications of her positions and to appear to occupy the ground of common sense.

Despite Butler's passionate and Davies's sarcastic attacks on justifications for women's educational inequality, they, like many feminist activists, remained to varying degrees attached to the vocabulary of domestic ideology, eschewing a more confrontational and directly political language of individual rights and demands. "You know of course," Davies wrote to one correspondent, objecting to a plan to endorse a "new, independent, female University," "that my feeling against raising barriers between men and women has nothing to do with the assertion of equality or identity, in neither of which I believe." Davies offers no explicit alternative to a belief in "equality and identity" as a motive for opposing a "*system* of separateness" (qtd. in Stephen, 195) and insisting that middle-class women should be given an education *equal* and *identical* to that of their male counterparts: her assurance seems to raise as many questions as it settles. Butler frequently called upon conventional distinctions between men's and women's "natures" to support her arguments for women's education:

> When a better education is secured to women . . . we may expect to find . . . that they will become the *more* and not the *less* womanly. Every good quality, every virtue which we regard as distinctively feminine, will, under conditions of greater freedom, develop more freely. . . . It will always be in [the woman's] nature to foster, to cherish, to take the part of the weak, to train, to guide, to have a care for individuals, to

discern the small seeds of a great future, to warm and cherish those seeds into fulness of life. "I serve" will always be one of her favourite mottos. (80)

In all her writing, Butler consistently celebrates marriage and family and represents her own active philanthropic career as nourished by the politics and support of both her father and her husband. Butler even defended single women, paradoxically, by assimilating them to married women: "We are all mothers or foster-mothers. . . . I have known many unmarried women in whom all the best characteristics are stronger than in some who are actually mothers. It would be wise of the State to avail itself to his abundance of generous womanliness" (81).

Davies too recognized her obligations to engage the concerns of domestic ideology, and she also asserted that educated women were more, rather than less, fit for marriage: "The enormous loss to general culture entailed by the solitude of the male intellect is very little thought of" (114), she writes: "It is in fact as a means of bringing men and women together, and bridging over the intellectual gulf between them, that a more liberal education and a larger scope for women are chiefly to be desired" (116–17). But her arguments on this point—very similar to those of Mill in *The Subjection of Women* (written in 1861, although not published until 1869)—have an air of distracted conventionality, and assort oddly with her proposal that professional women should continue to work after marriage, a possibility publicly espoused by few in the movement (and dismissed by Mill in *The Subjection of Women*) and one that cannot possibly have had a reassuring effect on conservative readers. Often, in fact, Davies seems barely able to contain her distaste for conventional family life. In "Home and the Higher Education," for example, she complains: "It is usual for the whole family to congregate in one room, each being alike the victim of every interruption, every one carrying on her individual occupation in suspense, so to speak, liable at any moment to be called off from it for something else, trifling or important, as the case may be. Naturally enough, these half occupied people prey upon each other" (119). To one correspondent she wrote even more frankly that "I do not believe that our utmost efforts to poison the students' lives at College will make them half so miserable as they are at home" (qtd. in Stephen, 174).

Reading the unpublished "Family Chronicle" that Davies wrote in her old age for the younger generations of her family, it is difficult not to conclude, as Caine does in her astute analysis of this work, that such attitudes reflected the "embittering nature of her own experience." In the "Family Chronicle," for example, she speculates that her father excluded girls from the school run by one of his curates "on the grounds that their presence would lower its status" (Caine, *Victorian Feminists,* 65, 62). Her summary of her own education is a succinct indictment of the midcentury education of middle-class girls:

> I went for a few months to a small day school for girls. Afterwards, I did some lessons with Jane [her sister]. We had lessons in French and Italian . . . and in music. Our education answered to the description of that of clergymen's daughters generally, given by Mark Pattison in his evidence to one of the Education Commissions. "Do they go to school? No. Do they have governesses at home? No. They have lessons and get on as they can." . . . I learnt a little Latin for my own pleasure, simply because the boys were doing it. . . . William and I used to do what were then called themes, i.e. bits of English composition, once a week, and the practice was no doubt very useful. ("Family Chronicle")

Perhaps a hint of sarcasm emerges in that last comment on theme writing, but the description otherwise maintains the deadpan style of the rest of the "Family Chronicle," whose lack of emotional evocation of any kind—affectionate or critical—is itself chilling. In this text, Davies adds pointed silence to the arsenal of rhetorical devices by which she calibrates and indicates her simultaneous distance from, and loyalty to, the domestic ideal.

In an 1865 letter to her colleague Barbara Bodichon about a paper on women's suffrage that Bodichon planned to give, Davies wrote

> I don't think it quite does to call the arguments on the other side "foolish." Of course they *are,* but it does not seem quite polite to say so. . . . The enemy always maintains that the disabilities imposed upon women are not penal, but solely intended for their good, and I find nothing irritates men so much as to attribute tyranny to them. I believe many of them

do really mean well, and at any rate as they say they do, it seems fair to admit it and to show them that their well intended efforts are a *mistake,* not a crime. . . . These papers travel about the country and go into families, where they may be read by prejudiced men. So it is necessary to be careful. (Qtd. in Stephen, 108)

Davies's analysis here is both frankly duplicitous, in calling on Bodichon to conceal the "foolishness" of the arguments on "the other side," and genuinely ambivalent: *Do* men "mean well," or do they (duplicitous in their turn) only "say they do"? Are men in fact the "enemy," engaged in "crime," or is "tyranny" merely an "attribut[ion]," a misreading of their "well intended efforts?"

The "disability" that Davies refers to here is women's exclusion from the suffrage, not from higher education. But the letter nevertheless illuminates the larger questions of substance and strategy that women in the higher education movement constantly faced: To what extent are the masculine and feminine roles of domestic ideology tyrannous? What part, if any, of their good intentions can be salvaged? How much duplicity is involved in the representation of domestic ideology's limitations as mistaken rather than criminal? And finally, what losses—for example, of familial connection—might be entailed by arraigning them? Such questions, underlying much of the rhetoric of the higher education movement, produced a range of split or doubled representations, from the tension in Shirreff's work between the expansiveness of mental cultivation and the narrowness of domestic life, to the tension in Butler's between the androgyny of spiritual, and the separate spheres of worldly, life, and the Girton students' parade of decorum as both a palliation of their transgression and an assertion of their seriousness. Davies's writing demonstrates an impressive and often conflicting range of rhetorical strategies that manage her doubled relationship to domestic ideology: from the internalized negotiations with patriarchal traditions of the letter with which I began to the overt recommendation of duplicity in the letter to Bodichon above; from the unlocalized agency of opposition in the published writing to the frank recognition of male "tyranny" in some of the letters; from sarcasm, on the one hand, to a tone of "calm good sense," on the other.

Like the activists in the higher education movement and their texts, the novelists and novels to which I now turn grapple with a conflict between indebtedness and opposition to the values of domestic ideology as they attempt to locate the intellectually ambitious woman in relation to those values.

Chapter 2

Living on the Moon
Jane Eyre and the Limits of Self-Education

Charlotte Brontë's *Jane Eyre* (1847) appeared at the outset of the movement for the reform of women's education: at the moment when attempts
to address the problems posed by the figure of the ill-trained and ill-paid
governess began to introduce ideas of reforming the higher education of
women. As Brontë in Yorkshire was writing to thank her publishers for six
complimentary copies of her first novel (Gérin, 338), the Christian Socialist reformer F. D. Maurice in London was organizing a series of evening
lectures to enable governesses to pass an examination that would win them
certificates and, the organizers hoped, thereby raise their status and salaries.
Out of these lectures grew Queen's and Bedford Colleges and ultimately
the movement for the higher education of women.[1] To this foundational
moment Brontë's relationship was at once removed and exemplary.

Brontë was removed from the roots of the higher education movement
by both geography and chronology. Regionally isolated, dead some twenty
years before Anne Clough's North of England Council for Promoting the
Higher Education of Women got underway with a series of lectures for
women in northern towns including Leeds and Manchester (Kamm, *Hope
Deferred,* 254), Brontë embodies its exigencies not by involvement with the

nascent movement, enthusiasm for its objects, or direct treatment of it in her fiction. Rather, Brontë's career is exemplary because it was defined by the conditions of intellectual ambition and labor for women that first made the movement a necessity: isolation and loneliness, drudgery, uncertainty.[2] Before the success of *Jane Eyre,* Brontë was one of the "hundreds and thousands of women, who, born in the middle class, live by its instruction . . . without any of that nicety of acquirement, or peculiar tact and science in imparting, which would enable them to outbid [their] hosts of sister governesses" (Parkes, "The Profession of the Teacher," 8). She attempted to improve these conditions for herself—she spent two years in Brussels, for example, bettering her French in hopes that the sisters would be able to open their own school, which never materialized (Gérin, 273–74).[3] Brontë's escape finally came not through the organized action that would mark the higher education movement but through an individual act of creative imagination—the transformation of her life struggles into fiction.

In this fiction Brontë creates not a fully articulated protest against the conditions that formed her but rather a vision of escape through the activity of intellect and imagination. From the outset, intellectual ability and ambition are the traits that distinguish Jane within her surroundings of deprivation, and *Jane Eyre* poses for its protagonist a series of alternative pedagogies by which to achieve that ambition. Schematically, these alternatives are the radical self-sufficiency of the autodidact; the intellectual and familial companionship of homosocial community; and the intellectual and erotic fulfillment of the heterosexual dyad. Even more schematically, we can associate these alternatives with ideologies that offered competing models of subjectivity: an entrenched domestic ideology and a nascent liberal individualism. In her self-sufficient isolation, Jane incarnates the apparently gender-neutral principles of liberal individualism, with its emphasis on the self-development of the subject and the rarity of "mental superiority" in the context of a "general tendency . . . to render mediocrity the ascendant power among mankind" (Mill, *On Liberty,* 66). The female intellectual communities in which Jane participates, on the other hand, embody familiar aspects of domestic ideology: its creation of a purely feminine and domestic space in opposition to the world of public endeavor and its subjection of individual intellectual capacity to larger social structures. Each of these alternatives, as I will argue, fails Jane, and her marriage to Edward Rochester reconciles them without fundamentally altering their competing imperatives.

The ambivalence of Brontë's location between the familiar comforts of the feminine subject of domestic ideology and the putatively gender-neutral subject of a nascent liberal individualism is legible in her response to an anonymous article that appeared in the *Westminster* in 1851, advocating women's suffrage, which she assumed was by John Stuart Mill, though she also confessed to first thinking it "the work of a powerful-minded, clear headed woman, who . . . longed for power, and had never felt affection." (Mill later attributed the essay to Harriet Taylor.) "Well-argued it is," she admitted:

> —clear, logical,—but vast is the hiatus of omission; harsh the consequent jar on every finer chord of the soul. . . . I think the author forgets there is such a thing as self-sacrificing love and disinterested devotion. . . . To many women affection is sweet, and power conquered indifferent—though we all like influence won. . . . In short, J. S. Mill's head is, I dare say, very good, but I feel disposed to scorn his heart. (Qtd. in Gaskell, 390)

This anxiety about a separation between the "heart," associated with women and with self-sacrifice, and the "head," associated with masculinity and with power, haunts *Jane Eyre* and weakens its impulse toward an individualist subjectivity that, at least as it is first incarnated in Rochester, seems to elevate logic and power over devotion and affection.

From the time that Elizabeth Rigby reviewed *Jane Eyre* along with the 1847 report of the Governesses' Benevolent Institution, taking the novel partly for a *roman à thèse* on the governess question and objecting that it was "far from beneficial to that class of ladies whose cause it affects to advocate" (176), Jane Eyre has taken her place in the parade of distressed gentlewomen who testify to the fascination of the nineteenth century—and of our own—with the challenge to Victorian class and gender organization that they signify.[4] But *Jane Eyre* differs from contemporary novels such as Harriet Martineau's *Deerbrook* (1839), in which the governess Maria Young silently sacrifices her hopes of love and marriage, and Anne Brontë's *Agnes Grey* (1847), which painstakingly details the humiliations visited on its gentle protagonist by both her employers and her charges, both of which depict governesses as simply overlooked and downtrodden. Jane hardly represents the pitiful "class of ladies" that Rigby finds in the pages of the 1847 report of the Governesses' Benevolent Institution, "all more or less reduced to indigence by the edifying fulfillment of their natural duties . . . after a life of labour and struggle" (183).[5]

It is true that Jane's salary of thirty pounds a year (93) falls well below the "hundred and twenty guineas" at which Rigby considers the governess "the cheapest luxury that can be had" (180), but she has no dependents to support, only one pupil, and the run of a large house. Although she famously experiences loneliness and ennui before the arrival of Rochester, pacing the leads and longing for "more of practical experience than I possessed; more of intercourse with my kind, of acquaintance with variety of character, than was here within my reach" (114), her relations with the other household dependents demonstrate none of the mutual scorn supposed to subsist between governesses and other servants. When Rochester does arrive, their "evening conferences" leave her "happy" and "gratified" (153)—contrary to Rigby's assertion that a governess is "a bore to almost any gentleman, as a tabooed woman, to whom he is interdicted from granting the usual privileges of the sex" (177). *Jane Eyre* is the story of a governess, but it is not being a governess that causes Jane difficulties. Rather, making Jane a governess—and one without family ties—allows Brontë to create a protagonist who has a mobility that, although limited, is greater than that of the usual heroine of the domestic novel,[6] while maintaining her claim to gentility and respectability. *Jane Eyre*—like the higher education movement itself—attempts to transform being a governess, a self-supporting middle-class woman, from a confession of failure to a condition of possibility. At the same time, however, that possibility is fulfilled only by the transformation of Jane herself from Rochester's employee and Adèle's governess to Rochester's wife and Adèle's mother. Brontë's recuperation of the meaning of the self-supporting middle-class woman, then—also like that of the early higher education movement—is only partial, continuing to take domesticity as its highest ideal.

Of the first two alternatives that the novel poses to Jane—the individualist trajectory of self-education and self-reliance, on the one hand, and the possibility of female intellectual community, on the other—it is the trajectory of self-education that appears first and dominates the narrative.[7] As Gayatri Spivak has observed, the opening of Jane's narrative is "a scene of the marginalization and privatization of the protagonist" in which we follow "the track of a unique imagination" (246) as Jane slips into the window seat with *Bewick's History of British Birds*. For Spivak, this "track" establishes the twentieth-century critical fascination with Jane's story as "the psychobiography of the militant female subject" (245), a reading that she revises by demonstrating that the construction of Jane as an individualist subject symmetrically depends on the construction of Bertha Mason, and the imperialist subjection she represents, as the "'native female' . . . [who] is excluded from any share in this emerging norm." Certainly Brontë, in *Jane Eyre* as in her other novels (particularly *Villette*), leans heavily on the distinction between English subjectivity, identified with the liberty of the individual, and foreign subjection, an undifferentiated category of immorality and coercion that includes not only the Creole Bertha Mason, but also Rochester's discarded continental mistresses, the women of the Turkish "seraglio" whom Jane accuses Rochester of desiring, and the Indian women to whom St. John Rivers invites her to minister. None of these figures is recuperated in the "emerging norm" of the liberty of the specifically *female* individual embodied in Jane Eyre. Nevertheless, I want to return to the "track" of Jane's imagination to suggest that the novel's complacency about its "axiomatics of imperialism" (Spivak, 247) is not matched by complacency about Jane's "unique" position as a proto-individualist subject.

Entering into the opening scene, we are in no doubt that it is Jane's salvation to be a reader rather than a Reed, drawing upon internal imaginative and intellectual resources, rather than bending in the wind of conventional attitudes and opinions. The robust, bourgeois Reeds are John Stuart Mill's nightmare of ascendant mediocrity, the antithesis of individual genius. By contrast, the books that Jane chooses, apparently fortuitously—*Bewick's History of British Birds*, Goldsmith's *History of Rome,* and Swift's *Gulliver's Travels*—have a coherent appeal: each transports Jane to some world of singularity and extremity. The "death-white realms" of Bewick's Antarctica (8); the despotism of "Nero, Caligula, &c." (11); the "little trees . . . the diminutive people" of Lilliput, and the "corn-fields forest-high . . . tower-like men and women" of Brobdingnag (21) remove her as far as possible from the diminished and diminishing setting of the Reed household, with its "leafless shrubbery," John Reed's petty terrorism, and Jane's unheroic "consciousness of physical inferiority" (7). These imaginative removes are the first of the journeys that Jane undertakes, and like the subsequent journeys—to Lowood, Thornfield, and Marsh End—they both endanger and liberate her. At Gateshead, her imagination endangers her because her absorption in Bewick becomes the pretext for John Reed's wrath and her immurement in the red room. But the breakdown in the red room and succeeding events ultimately decide Mrs. Reed to send Jane away to school; it is, therefore, Jane's own imaginative power that enables her escape from Gateshead and her first steps toward greater knowledge and experience.

This pattern is repeated throughout the novel. Each of Jane's forays into new territory, in search of "real knowledge of life" (88), depends on the promptings of imagination. Searching for the means of leaving Lowood after the departure of her mentor, Miss Temple, Jane thinks "the end is not so difficult; if I had only a brain active enough to ferret out the means of attaining it," and her brain obliges with a suggestion that "came quietly and naturally to my mind:—'Those who want situations advertise'" (90). Jane remains quick to assert the primacy and singularity of her imagination. When Rochester, for instance, asks if a drawing-master helped her with the sketches he has seen, she denies it emphatically (130). From this perspective, Jane's narrative trajectory appears to be that of the self-taught, self-sustaining female individualist.

Sharon Marcus, however, has persuasively argued that Jane Eyre's use of the anonymous and self-alienating medium of advertisement, and of writing in general, displaces rather than expresses her agency: "Jane uses the medium of the written advertisement to negotiate between absolute self-effacement, represented by Helen Burns, and spectacular, Byronic embodiment, personified by Rochester" (209)—or, in the terms of my argument, between the self-denial of domestic ideology and the self-assertion of liberal individualism. More generally, for all Jane's pride in the suggestions of her imagination, she remains reluctant to claim them as fully hers. Indeed, as the novel progresses and the situations in which she must rely upon an inner voice to direct her become more and more critical, she shows a greater impulse to disown that voice. An initial suggestion about her decision to advertise for a position—that "a kind fairy, in my absence" has "dropped the required suggestion on my pillow" (90)—is jocular. But the voice that prompts her to flee Rochester after his treachery is revealed comes distinctly from outside her, although in a form of whose materiality some doubt remains: "not a moon, but a white human form shone in the azure. . . . It spoke, to my spirit . . . it whispered in my heart—'My daughter, flee temptation!'" (337). The voice that urges her to return to him as she struggles with St. John Rivers's proposal is less material—"I saw nothing: but I heard a voice somewhere cry—'Jane! Jane! Jane!'" (442) but proves even more demonstrably to have originated from without, as words that "broke involuntarily from [Rochester's] lips" at precisely the same time that Jane hears them (471). Brontë celebrates the force of Jane's imagination—"It was *my* turn to assume ascendancy. *My* powers were in play" (442), Jane exults after hearing Rochester's cry—but she neither, as a result, represents Jane as fully autonomous, nor condemns her to complete isolation. When Jane lacks human interlocutors, these phantasms in some degree compensate for her isolation.[8]

The possibility that the virtue of self-reliance may become the torture of isolation continually shadows the trajectory of Jane's independence. After Jane leaves Gateshead for Lowood, her fellow pupils and her teachers, with the exceptions of Helen Burns and Miss Temple, confirm her in her feelings of lonely superiority to her surroundings. The teachers are abusive, like Miss Scatcherd, the shrill tormentor of Helen Burns, or repellent, like Miss Gryce, the "heavy Welshwoman" whose "habitual nasal strains" disturb Jane's nighttime thoughts after she has become a teacher herself. A similar revulsion appears in *Villette,* where Lucy Snowe dismisses her colleagues in a brief passage:

> I lived in a house full of robust life; I might have had companions, and I chose solitude. . . . One [teacher] I found to be an honest woman, but a narrow thinker, a coarse feeler, and an egotist. The second was a Parisienne, externally refined—at heart, corrupt—without a creed, without a principle, without an affection. . . . [The third] had also one other distinctive property—that of avarice. (155)[9]

Helena Michie has pointed to relations among women that she names "sororophobia"—"the negotiation of sameness and difference, identity and separation, between women of the same generation . . . [encompassing] both the desire for and the recoil from identification with other women" (9). Jane's recoil from women who share her socioeconomic circumstances clearly proceeds as much from a rejection of those circumstances as from actual attributes of the women themselves, who are, indeed, barely characterized. The recoil response expresses Jane's determination not to become trapped in the "school-rules, school duties, school-habits and notions, and voices, and faces, and phrases, and costumes, and preferences, and antipathies" (89) that she associates with her fellow teachers—to retain her uniqueness. At the same time, however, it condemns her to intellectual and social isolation.[10] Even Thornfield in its master's absence, as Jane first experiences it, exists in suspension, Mrs. Fairfax dusting and airing unused rooms in anticipation of Rochester's visits. Between Mrs. Fairfax's amiable vacuity and Adèle's precocious coquetry, Grace Poole's coarseness and porter drinking and the disembodied and terrifying laugh that represents Bertha Rochester, Thornfield's feminine possibilities range from an overt ennui to a hidden madness, and once again, Jane keeps herself aloof from them, turning instead to the compensatory resources of her own imagination: "My sole relief was to walk along the corridor of the third story . . . and allow my mind's eye to dwell on whatever bright visions rose before it . . . and best of all, to open my inward ear to a tale that was never ended" (114).[11]

But the rejection that preserves Jane's sense of uniqueness also condemns her to intellectual and social isolation; reciprocally, her enforced reliance on her own imagination creates a closed circle of narrative that does nothing to connect her to the wider world of knowledge and experience for which she longs. As one potential solution to this isolation, Brontë offers a homosocial, female intellectual community that might sustain rather than entrap Jane.[12] *Jane Eyre* offers two examples of such community: first, Jane's childhood idyll with Helen Burns and Miss Temple at Lowood; second, her sojourn with Diana and Mary Rivers at Marsh End. In both cases, Jane is succored both physically and intellectually by women to whom she plays the role of the admiring disciple; in both cases, the potential erotics of the connection take the form of familial relations; and in both cases, the community proves transitory, weakened from without by patriarchal imposition, dissolved from within by its members' acquiescence to their own roles within that patriarchal structure.

I said above that the narrative of Jane as a self-reliant subject begins with her solitary, imaginative retreat into the curtained window seat and the "death-white realms" of Bewick. But that scene of "double retirement" is actually the outcome of a prior scene, of exclusion: "[Mrs. Reed] lay reclined on a sofa by the fire-side, and with her darlings about her (for the time neither quarrelling nor crying) looked perfectly happy," but Jane has been "dispensed from joining the group" until she can "acquire a more sociable and child-like disposition" (7). This scene is a travesty of the kind of maternal, moral tuition envisioned by the domestic ideal. Mrs. Reed is not Jane's mother and refuses to act the part of one toward her. The image of the apparently happy family group conceals hypocrisy, bullying, and neglect.

And despite Mrs. Reed's apparent centrality to the scene and the character that Jane gives her elsewhere, of being "an exact, clever manager, her household and tenantry . . . thoroughly under her control" (37), the household organization is not matriarchal but patriarchal: "[A]ll the house belongs to me, or will do in a few years" as John Reed tells Jane (11).

At Lowood, under the protection of the superintendent, Miss Temple, and Jane's fellow student, Helen Burns, Jane recuperates that earlier experience of exclusion from the fireside family group at Gateshead in a different fireside scene. Both Helen Burns and Miss Temple come to comfort Jane after Brocklehurst denounces her to the school as a liar, and Miss Temple brings the two girls up to her room. That evening, Jane observes Helen:

> The refreshing meal, the brilliant fire, the presence and kindness of her beloved instructress, or perhaps more than all these, something in her own unique mind, had roused [Helen's] powers within her. They woke, they kindled: first, they glowed in the bright tint of her cheek, which till this hour I had never seen but pale and bloodless; then they shone in the liquid lustre of her eyes.

In this scene, although Jane remains a watcher, she is invited to, rather than excluded from, the fireside, and Miss Temple has the power to "satisfy [the girls'] famished appetites on the delicate fare she liberally supplied" (76). The physical succor so absent at Gateshead remains central to this triangulated relationship: in the two short chapters that narrate the friendship between Jane and Helen, they nourish each other and are nourished by Miss Temple (Helen brings Jane food, Miss Temple gives the two girls both cake), offer each other physical comfort (Jane begins chapter 8 in Helen's arms and ends chapter 9 in bed beside her), and are physically comforted by Miss Temple (Helen breathes her last in Miss Temple's room). While it might be possible to read a protolesbian erotics into the physical intimacy and emotional arousal of these passages, their libidinal energy seems to flow more in the direction of the family romance: Miss Temple is the nurturing mother Jane has not had, and Helen is the consoling sister, while the patriarchal dependence of which Jane has had such unhappy experience is, in this scene, altogether suppressed.

Although the fantasy of physical succor may be essentially a child's, the intellectual rapport between Miss Temple and Helen, which Jane observes with wistful astonishment, adumbrates her later pleasure in intellectual discipleship:

> They conversed of things I had never heard of; of nations and times past; of countries far away; of secrets of nature discovered or guessed at: they spoke of books: how many they had read! What stores of knowledge they possessed! . . . [M]y amazement reached its climax when Miss Temple . . . taking a book from a shelf, bade [Helen] read and construe a page of Virgil; and Helen obeyed. (76)

As in her reading at Lowick, Jane is here most impressed by the power of the intellect to provide routes of escape: "nations and times past . . . countries far away . . . secrets of nature discovered or guessed at." It is always the not-yet-known that captures her imagination.

But such forms of escape are limited, and this female community proves to be as much mirage as oasis, unstable and limited in its encounter with patriarchal regulation. Lowood has its John Reed. The generosity that moves Miss Temple to augment a school breakfast of burnt porridge with a lunch of bread and cheese draws a swift rebuke from Brocklehurst (66). Similarly, although Miss Temple ruefully monitors Helen's consumptive decline, she cannot prevent her death, or the outbreak of typhoid that follows it. The "serenity in [Miss Temple's] air, . . . state in her mien . . . [and] refined propriety in her language" (76) mark her as the true woman of the domestic ideal, but she is also limited by those traits. When, after ten years, marriage removes the maternal Miss Temple from Jane to her proper domestic place as inevitably as a beautiful death removed Helen, her influence proves remarkably transitory. By the end of the day of her departure, Jane realizes that "my mind had put off all it had borrowed of Miss Temple . . . and that now I was left in my natural element, and beginning to feel the stirring of old emotions." Liberated from Brocklehurst's patriarchal rule, Lowood and Jane flourish under Miss Temple's maternal guidance; but Miss Temple's departure immediately reveals Lowood's community of teachers and students to Jane as static and narrow, a world of "rules and systems" to be left as soon as possible for the "varied field of hopes and fears" (88) for which she longs, and which it remains for Rochester to provide.

The same impermanence marks the novel's second succoring sisterhood—Diana and Mary Rivers. Taken in by the Riverses, Jane becomes again the disciple of female intellect, this time able to take a more active intellectual role: "They were both more accomplished and better read than I was: but with eagerness I followed in the path of knowledge they had trodden before me. I devoured the books they lent me: then it was full satisfaction to discuss with them in the evening what I had perused during the day." More markedly than in the childhood scene, the scene hints at erotic possibility:

> If in our trio there was a superior and a leader, it was Diana. Physically, she far excelled me: she was handsome; she was vigorous. In her animal spirits there was an affluence of life. . . . [T]he first gush of [my] vivacity gone, I was fain to sit on a stool at Diana's feet, to rest my head on her knee. . . . I liked to learn of her: I saw the part of instructress pleased and suited her; that of scholar pleased and suited me no less. Our natures dovetailed: mutual affection—of the strongest kind—was the result. (369)

But once again, and more explicitly, libidinal energies are directed into ties of kinship. On finding out simultaneously that she is an heiress and that the Riverses are her kin, Jane rejoices that "the two girls, on whom . . . I had gazed with so bitter a mixture of interest and despair, were my near kinswomen; and the young and stately gentleman who had found me almost dying at his threshold, was my blood relation" (405). Indeed, it is the wealth that comes with this revelation that enables Jane to resist the burlesque of erotic connection that her new home does offer: St. John's insistence that she enter into a passionless marriage with him that will annex her to his ambitions as a missionary wife.

My point here is not that Jane's connection to Diana is "really" erotic, or that it should have been; but rather, that the lack of possibility (as she understands it) for a fully realized erotic connection is part of what makes Brontë's female homosocial communities unsustainable, and unimaginable except in familial terms.[13] Even economic self-determination cannot compensate for this absence. The family's financial situation, which forces Diana and Mary to go out as governesses, is a result of patriarchal economics: their uncle has chosen to leave his fortune to another relation (who turns out, of course, to be Jane); and as Diana observes, "He had a right . . . to do as he pleased" (377). When Jane inherits this money, she also, as a single woman, has a right to do as she pleases with it. Choosing to share it with the Riverses, she releases Diana and Mary from the need to work, but ironically that release only hastens the final dispersal of this second female community, for the girls are now enabled to marry. Between the cruel economics and the compelling erotics (in Brontë's view) of patriarchal organization, female homosocial communities have little chance of survival. The closure of marriage obliterates the female intellectual companionship that in any case exists only in diaspora, preliminary to the happy translation of marriage (in the cases of Miss Temple and the Rivers sisters) or the melancholy translation of death (in the case of Helen Burns).

The second solution that Brontë proposes for Jane's isolation, then, is that of a more explicitly eroticized pedagogy in the form of a male/female instructor/disciple dyad. This relationship is characterized by a reduplicative hierarchical structure in which the female disciple is paired with an instructor who is not only male, but also older, more experienced, and more financially secure; and by an erotic tension that functions to transform the instructor/disciple relationship into a more conventional husband/wife dyad. This last point is particularly important, since it enables the relationship to take on the permanence denied to women's intellectual communities. This structure is not confined to *Jane Eyre;* Brontë also explores its possibilities in the relationships between William Crimsworth and Frances Henri in *The Professor,* Louis Moore and Shirley Keeldar in *Shirley;* and Paul Emmanuel and Lucy Snowe in *Villette.*

The unfolding of such an erotic pedagogy dominates the middle part of *Jane Eyre.* Rochester claims over Jane "such superiority as must result from twenty years' difference in age and a century's advance in experience" (139), and she herself reminds him of her dependency as a "paid subordinate" (140). She submits herself to his instruction in "scenes and ways" (153) as a strikingly willing pupil: "I had a keen delight in receiving the new ideas he offered, in imaging [*sic*] the new pictures he portrayed, and following him in thought through the new regions he disclosed" (153). Jane believes that she is discovering that knowledge of the world for which she longs; but the gerundive verbs of this passage—"receiving," "imaging," "following"—emphasize receptivity, not active discovery: the scene represents a diminution of Jane's earlier longing for a "power of vision which might overpass [the] limit" of the horizon (114). Flattered and fed by Rochester's attention—"The confidence he had thought fit to repose in me seemed a tribute to my discretion. . . . I was honoured by a cordiality of reception that made me feel I really possessed the power to please him" (153)—Jane does not notice that she is still "follow[ing] another's thought," rather than actually encountering "new regions."

The scene of instruction/seduction is not, however, entirely, or not only, one of masculine assertion and feminine sensibility. For Brontë, the erotics of pedagogy depend on a shifting power dynamic in which the female disciple intermittently displays her capacity for resistance and evaluation. This resistance also preserves a moral dimension within the erotic connection: "If I bid you to do what you thought wrong," Rochester observes presciently, "[my] friend would then turn to me, quiet and pale, and would say, 'No, sir; that is impossible: I cannot do it, because it is wrong'" (227–28). The greatest scorn of Brontë's teachers is reserved for students who display "mere undisciplined disaffection and wanton indocility" (*Villette*, 101), rather than this principled resistance. Thus Jane disclaims Rochester's "right to command me, merely because you are older than I, or because you have seen more of the world than I have," insisting that his "command" must depend upon "the use you have made of your time and experience" (139). And she asserts her right to instruct him morally in imperative terms. When he presses her, in enigmatic language, to approve his "right to get pleasure out of life . . . cost what it may" (142), she rebukes him with a forcefulness scarcely disguised by her insistence on addressing him as "sir": "Then you will degenerate still more, sir"; "[Pleasure] will sting—it will taste bitter, sir"; "Distrust it, sir; it is not a true angel" (143). Although Rochester protests that Jane has "no right to preach to me; you Neophyte, that have not passed the porch of life, and are absolutely unacquainted with its mysteries" (143), he will much later admit the justice of her views: "I did wrong: I would have sullied my innocent flower—breathed guilt on its purity: the Omnipotent snatched it from me" (470). It is Rochester's confession of his error and Jane's truth, as much as the reduction of his physical and economic power in relation to her, that allows them to be united on equal terms.[14]

But Rochester's is not the only error that must be overcome on the way to this resolution. Despite her principled resistance, "I was growing very lenient to my master," Jane confesses: "I was forgetting all his faults, for which I had once kept a sharp look-out. . . . And as for the vague something . . . which used to make me fear and shrink. . . . Instead of wishing to shun, I longed only to dare—to divine it" (197–98). The fact is that Rochester's scene of instruction is from the beginning a scene of seduction, and Jane's protestation that she is "never startled or troubled by one noxious allusion" rings hollow in its attempt to dismiss the erotic implications of their conversations, which begin, after all, with an erotic fairy-tale—the history of Rochester's relations with Céline Varens.

Jane's relationship with Rochester, therefore, must evolve from one of discipleship to one of discipline. The crisis point of the novel at which this evolution occurs—the point at which Rochester's treachery is revealed and Jane resolves to leave him rather than live as his mistress—has often been read as a crisis in Brontë's own narration.[15] Simply put, Jane's behavior seems morally and psychologically inconsistent. The track of the "unique imagination" that we, up to this point, have been following has emphasized individualism and self-reliance: in balking at Rochester's agonized appeal and her own frankly avowed desire, Jane seems to sink to a narrow compliance with what Rochester dismissively calls "early instilled prejudice." Twentieth-century feminist readings have tended to recuperate this decision within the psychological terms of individualism itself, viewing it as "the first crucial step toward independence"; "rebellion against Rochester's arrogance"; or "the instinct toward self-preservation."[16] Each of these explanations is psychologically plausible, but their attempts to keep Jane's behavior coherently within the terms of a project of individualist self-development subtly alter the way in which ideas such as "independence" "rebellion," and "self-preservation" have functioned in the previous trajectory of the novel; they minimize the shocking abruptness of the intervention of social and religious orthodoxy; and they overlook or discount the form of Jane's act of self-assertion—her insistence on the value of her chastity—which is culturally most legible as submission to patriarchal law.

In fact, rather than continuing to demonstrate an unquestioning adherence to individualist norms, Jane here comes up against the limits of an attempt to apply the model of liberal individualism to a female subject as though she were living in a gender-neutral society. Margaret Homans observes that "in the nineteenth century, women did nothing, including writing, except as women" (*Bearing the Word,* 29). Brontë recognizes that truth of gender; but for most of Jane's first-person narrative she evades rather than challenges it. Sandra M. Gilbert and Susan Gubar refer to Jane Eyre's struggles as "symptomatic of difficulties Everywoman in a patriarchal society must meet and overcome" (339), but one imagines that Jane might have preferred G. H. Lewes's characterization of her as "a struggling, suffering, much enduring human spirit" (691)—that is to say, as "human" rather than "woman." Jane rarely draws attention to the fact of her femaleness, which the first-person pronoun allows her to downplay.[17] The endearments of Rochester's that she most appreciates, indeed, locate her in a realm where human gender is invisible: she is an "elf" (257, 329); his "fairy" (281, 460); a "ministrant spirit" (214). This is the promise of individualism—the promise of a realm where desire is not confined by gender or by other ascriptive traits. When Rochester begins to use more conventional terms of endearment that refer to Jane's sex—"girl-bride" (271); "beauty"; "angel"(272)— and as he showers her with seigniorial gifts, such as jewels and gowns, that themselves emphasize her femininity, she becomes restive: "Glad I was to get him out of the silk warehouse, and then out of a jeweller's shop: the more he bought me, the more my cheeks burned with a sense of annoyance and degradation" (281). Jane intuits that Rochester's recognition of her as a woman can only work to her disadvantage. Even at this point, however, Jane implicitly assigns her discomfort to the inequality in their financial situations, rather than a gender imbalance, resolving to write to her Madeira uncle: "If I had but a prospect of one day bringing Mr. Rochester an accession of fortune, I could better endure to be kept by him now" (281–82).

In his argument to Jane about why she should live with him as his mistress, Rochester turns upon her the apparently gender-neutral language of individualism: "And what a distortion in your judgment, what a perversity in your ideas, is proved by your conduct! Is it better to drive a fellow-creature to despair than to transgress a mere human law, no man being injured by the breach?—for you have neither relatives nor acquaintances whom you need fear to offend by living with me" (334). On the face of it, Rochester has every reason to expect that this argument will sway Jane, who, in declaring her love for him, asserts: "I am not talking to you now through the medium of custom, conventionalities, nor even of mortal flesh: it is my spirit that addresses your spirit; just as if both had passed through the grave, and we stood at God's feet, equal,—as we are!" (266). At this moment of crisis—when a real, rather than a vicarious, experience of "the storms of an uncertain struggling life" (122) opens up before her—Jane seems to fall back upon precisely such gendered "customs [and] conventionalities" as her previous behavior has flouted. Rochester's confusion is surely understandable, but his own assumptions are equally gendered and hardly neutral.

Rochester's behavior reveals a masculine arrogation of power beneath the apparently gender-neutral vocabulary of individualism. First, his breathlessly legalistic, and hardly tactful, aside, "you have neither relatives nor acquaintances whom you need fear to offend" serves to remind Jane that her personal value is defined, as much for Rochester as for more conventional suitors, not by her worth as an individual, but by her place in familial and social structures: what makes her available to Rochester is her lack of such standing. His calculating awareness of her circumstances underscores her similarity to his discarded mistresses and imprisoned wife: all are dependent and unprotected, liable to be seduced, lied to, and controlled by men of substance.[18] "To live familiarly with inferiors is degrading," says Rochester of his previous mistresses, and Jane "drew from [these words] the certain inference, that if I were so far to forget myself . . . as . . . to become the successor of these poor girls, he would one day regard me with the same feeling which now in his mind desecrated their memory" (329). Even on its most favorable interpretation, Rochester's offer—"You shall go to a place I have in the south of France: a white-walled villa on the shores of the Mediterranean. There you shall live a happy, and guarded, and most innocent life" (320)—is a tender of bondage, not a liberation from custom into agency, since Jane in these circumstances would be totally dependent on Rochester's financial and social protection. Finally, the words "no *man* being injured in the breach" (emphasis added) draw attention to the fact that it is Rochester, the man of property, who has least to lose by engaging in irregularities that are winked at by the custom of the double standard operating with regard to both gender and class.

In this crisis, then, Jane (and Brontë) reach the limit of a feminist individualism that imagines slipping gender's bonds rather than reforming its concrete social manifestations. In Rochester, before his repentance, a principled emphasis on personal will collapses into to the pure solipsism of libertinism. Jane responds to Rochester:

> "The more solitary, the more friendless, the more unsustained
> I am, the more I will respect myself. I will keep the law given
> by God; sanctioned by man. . . . If at my individual conven-
> ience I might break [these laws], what would be their worth?
> . . . . Preconceived opinions, foregone determinations are all I
> have at this hour to stand by; there I plant my foot." (344)

Jane here values "preconceived opinions [and] foregone determinations"—for which she has not previously shown any particular fondness—less for their particular moral content than their impersonality: the "law given by God [and] sanctioned by man" connects her to social structures larger than her "individual conscience." Jane rejects Rochester's masculine, aristocratic indifference to the existence and value of those structures. But she does not by that token experience any sudden conversion to the purely self-sacrificial implications of domestic ideology: she does not regret her passion or blame herself for her narrow escape. After St. John Rivers finds her employment, she congratulates herself on finding herself "a village-school-mistress, free and honest, in a breezy mountain nook in the healthy heart of England" (379). She also, however, finds herself lonely; within a paragraph of this self-congratulation, she is in tears.

At this point in the novel, it seems that each of the antidotes to Jane's isolation that Brontë has proposed has failed: reliance upon the "unique imagination," homosocial community, erotic heterosexual pedagogy. The task of the remainder of the novel—the third volume—will be to rehabilitate the last of these options. This trajectory entails a number of compromises. In particular, Jane's marriage to Rochester on terms that contravene neither social law nor Jane's narrative of self-reliance depends upon several notoriously fortuitous circumstances: the fire that kills Bertha and maims Rochester, and the revelation of Jane's inheritance. These events create structural, psychological, and ideological tensions. Structurally, they weight the last part of the book heavily toward a melodrama that undermines the narrative's dominant mode of realism; psychologically, they are at odds with the self-determining trajectory of Jane's narrative; ideologically, they call upon particularly repressive social forces such as imperialism (in Spivak's reading) or the renunciation of female anger (in Gilbert and Gubar's) in order to bring about Jane's ascendancy.

These tensions generally highlight the willed escapism of the novel's happy ending. There are other aspects of its resolution that more directly undermine the role of what I have called erotic pedagogy as a compromise between the individualist values of Jane's trajectory of self-education and self-reliance and domestic ideology's emphasis on female self-denial and conformity. The first is the relationship that Jane develops to her pupil, and later stepdaughter, Adèle Varens. When Jane meets her, Adèle is, like Jane herself, a child both orphaned and disowned: her mother, the French dancer with whom Rochester had an affair, is dead. Rochester dismisses his possible paternity, seeing "no proofs . . . written in her countenance" (151), and Jane declares that Adèle's parentless state will cause her "to cling closer to her than before" (152). In fact, however, her "cool" attitude to Adèle remains much the same as she describes it at their first acquaintance, before she has this information: "She made reasonable progress, entertained for me a vivacious, though perhaps not very profound affection, and by her simplicity, gay prattle, and efforts to please, inspired me, in return, with a degree of attachment sufficient to make us both content in each other's society" (113). If this is a warmer degree of attachment than Mrs. Reed demonstrated for Jane, it is hardly an ideal maternal devotion. If Rochester denies any physical resemblance to Adèle, Jane seems equally eager to preclude the possibility of any identity between Adèle and herself based on their resemblance of situation. Where the child Jane was a "heterogeneous thing" (16), Adèle has "no great talents, no marked traits of character"; Jane is "obliged to be plain—for I had no article of attire that was not made with extreme simplicity" (103), and she finds something "ludicrous as well as painful . . . [in Adèle's] earnest and innate devotion to matters of dress" (179). In every point, Jane distinguishes both her child and her adult self from the precociously feminine Adèle.

In Adèle the desires that also move Jane—"I ever wished to look as well as I could, and to please as much as my want of beauty would permit" (103), she owns—become trivial. Where the child Jane exclaims that "to gain some real affection from . . . any[one] whom I truly love, I would willingly submit to have the bone of my arm broken, or to let a bull toss me, or to stand behind a kicking horse, and let it dash its hoof at my chest" (72), Adèle is content with such regard from Rochester as can be demonstrated by "cadeaux." In Adèle, in fact, the continental coquette—the "other" woman—appears in diminished form. Her role in the narrative at first seems to be simply to allow Jane to fulfill the mandate of cultural dissemination that unites the English governess and the English mother, by turning that "genuine daughter of Paris" into a docile daughter of Albion. For Adèle's precocious sensuality and materialism are apparently both national and (like Bertha Mason's) hereditary. Although she has been taken out of the "slime and mud of Paris, and transplanted . . . to grow up clean in the wholesome soil of an English country garden," she displays a congenital interest in clothing, "cadeaux," and flirtation, as well as a "superficiality of character, inherited probably from her mother, hardly congenial to an English mind" (176). Once "committed entirely to [Jane's] care," however,

Adèle soon "forg[ets] her little freaks, and bec[omes] obedient and teach-able" (140). When Jane becomes Adèle's stepmother, she ceases to be her governess; but once again she steps in judiciously to remove Adèle from the "too severe" school in which the inattentive Rochester (lacking Jane's ma-ternal insight) has placed her. Adèle's story closes with a paean to the effects of a "sound English education . . . [that] corrected in a great measure her French defects." Jane concludes Adèle's narrative with praise not much stronger than that with which she began: "[W]hen she left school, I found in her a pleasing and obliging companion—docile, good-tempered, and well-principled" (475). Jane's conversion of Adèle to a docility that she her-self, as a child, utterly repudiated, and particularly her insistent denial of the sexuality with which Adèle is associated, is chilling. If Adèle's child-hood rewrites Jane's, it is Jane's passionate "heterogeneity," rather than her loneliness, that is thereby diminished.[19]

Jane's disciplinary relationship to Adèle thus both inserts Jane in the role of domesticator and, retroactively, domesticates her. It is a fantasized close to her own story that, ignoring that story's actual trajectory, belongs to the realm of pure (domestic) ideology. Jane's desire is redirected through the convention of "woman's mission": the superintendence and embodi-ment of respectable morality that, as much as or more than education, was the governess's primary function. But this fantasy remains tangential to the ending of *Jane Eyre;* by encapsulating the plot of taming and docility in Adèle's story, Brontë expresses but also minimizes the most coercive and least subversive solution to the "problem" of Jane's desire. Adèle, after all, is banished from Ferndean, diminishing the constructed family and leaving Rochester and Jane together as a perpetual honeymoon couple (albeit joined in a vague future by a nameless heir).

Finally, it is questionable whether the reduced and isolated family struc-ture Brontë represents as *Jane Eyre*'s end point can be taken either as an emblem of a larger social world or as mediating between the individual sub-ject and the aggregate of other subjects. So intense is the mutuality that Jane and Rochester achieve that she can render it only through paralepsis:

> I know what it is to live entirely for and with what I love best
> on earth. I hold myself supremely blest—blest beyond what
> language can express; because I am my husband's life as fully
> as he is mine. . . . We talk, I believe, all day long: to talk to each
> other is but a more animated and an audible thinking. All my

confidence is bestowed on him; all his confidence is devoted to me: we are precisely suited in character; perfect concord is the result. (475)

Like Jane's insistence on Adèle's complete docility, her emphasis on "perfect concord" has a more chilling than reassuring effect, suggesting as it does that conflict can be avoided only by absolute assimilation, as though the ideal marriage in fact embodies only one identity, whose gender remains obscure. Brontë's representation of Jane and Rochester as interdependent subjects questions simultaneously the assumption of domestic ideology that women (only) are "relative creatures" and the implication of individualism at its most atomistic that anyone, man or woman, can be entirely independent. But the fusion of Jane and Rochester is so extreme as to make them essentially one individual—although that individual, contra the law of coverture, is (inasmuch as it is her story we hear, through the power of her voice) Jane, rather than Rochester; which is to say an individual who has internalized the conflict between desire and submission.[20] Jane Rochester thus might be said to represent a self-reconciliation but not a reconciliation of individual with social impulses. Blotting out society altogether, this solipsism "resolves" the competing claims of self and others in a way that is scarcely reproducible; certainly, it cannot be institutionalized, made publicly available.

Indeed, Brontë dismisses institutions early in the novel, when Jane, reading the "stone tablet" over Lowood's door, asks Helen Burns, "Why do they call [Lowood] Institution? Is it in any way different from other schools?" (52). Helen explains: "All the girls here have lost either one or both parents, and this is called an Institution for educating orphans" (52). Brontë makes the term refer to Lowood's foundations in a loss of family that—as Jane's subsequent experience of Lowood demonstrates—can be mitigated only incompletely by its intervention.

Jane Eyre's conclusion resembles the conciliatory conclusions of contemporary narratives motivated by female intellectual ambition. Tennyson's *The Princess,* for example, published in the same year as *Jane Eyre,* concludes with the prince's peroration: "The woman's cause is man's; they rise or sink / Together, dwarf'd or godlike, bond or free," he assures Princess Ida, and "in the long years liker must they grow," a process which will include a gain of "mental breadth" for the woman (VII, 243–44, 263, 267). Elizabeth Barrett Browning's *Aurora Leigh* (1857), which is indebted to both Brontë and Tennyson, similarly concludes with a rapprochement between its male and female protagonists, as the artist, Aurora, and the social reformer, Romney, trade confessions of inadequacy and vow to unite their respective strengths so that "our work shall still be better for our love, / And still our love be sweeter for our work" (350). Each of these visions of harmony, however, has its limits. Tennyson's prince has just razed the women's university established by Princess Ida. Romney has been blinded in the torching of his estate, on which he had attempted to establish a Fourierist commune, and Barrett Browning—less forgiving thanBrontë of masculine overreaching—intimates no restoration of his sight. In both cases, too, the social idealist partner is chastened into realizing the inadequacy—if not the futility—of her or his social activism: "fewer programmes . . . / Fewer systems . . . / Less mapping out of masses, to be saved, / By nations or by sexes" (348), promises Romney.

Among their other implications, these conclusions insist that the "work" of the artist, like the role of the woman within domestic ideology, is more contemplative than active. They valorize art as what Eliot later calls "the highest form of teaching," while preserving a status quo that makes the public roles of artist and intellectual, and the educational institutions that often produce them, more available to men than to women.[21] If Browning and Tennyson reject public and political solutions, however, both nevertheless conclude with more legible gestures toward the social world than Brontë reaches. Where the prince and Princess Ida come to represent complementary halves of one social organism, and Aurora and Romney similarly embody competing—but finally reconciled—ideals of social regeneration, Rochester and Jane instead embody conflicting interpretations of individualism itself. Rochester recognizes no social claims ("Your station is in my heart, and on the necks of those who would insult you" [276] he tells Jane at one point); Jane's recognition of them is partial and often resentful. Because Jane occupies both positions in the conflict between the potential lawlessness of self-fulfillment and the actual constraint of social responsibility—sometimes, as on the leads at Thornfield, she represents a unregenerate desire chafing against social law; at other times, as in her relationship to Adèle, she represents the subduing claims of society—both become aspects of her interior struggle. In the novel's attempt to reconcile these positions, that interior becomes the predominant location of a moral activity that cannot be externalized and is not amenable to political amelioration.

Early in his engagement to Jane, Rochester spins for Adèle a fantasy of his imminent marriage: "I am to take mademoiselle to the moon, and there I shall seek a cave in one of the white valleys among the volcano-tops, and mademoiselle shall live there with me, and only me" (279). The pragmatic Adèle anticipates that "[Jane] would get tired of living with only you on the moon" (280), but the novel's closing image of the Rochesters suggests that lunar isolation suits them nicely. The competing models of the social self— the implicitly feminine self whose identity is predicated on its own denial, and the implicitly masculine self whose identity is predicated on its own desires—present in the novel can, it seems, be united only within a social world reduced to little more than an effect of the protagonist's interiority. Jane's intellectual achievements at Lowood and her adoption of the role of educator lead her not into the public and institutional world but triumphantly back to the private and domestic one.

Chapter 3

From English Governess to Orientalist Scholar

Female Pedagogy and Power in Anna Leonowens's
The English Governess at the Siamese Court

According to her most recent biographer, Anna Harriette Leonowens (1831–1915) was born "on a tiny cot at the back of a stifling hot East India Company barracks on November 6, 1831," the posthumous daughter of an enlisted soldier, and most likely educated in a garrison school. She died eighty-four years later in upper-class comfort in Montreal, a noted local lecturer, travel writer, suffragist, and philanthropist; author of four books on Asian cultures, and the widow, according to her obituary in the *Montreal Star,* of one Major Leonowens (Dow, 1, 3, 138). She might have faded into history as a strong-minded matron of local renown, but for the fact that in her first book, *The English Governess at the Siamese Court* (1870), she created a governess heroine whose afterlife, as "Mrs. Anna" of twentieth-century stage and screen, has given her an iconic stature surpassing even Jane Eyre's. Some thirty years after her death, Leonowens's Siam memoirs, *The English Governess* and *The Romance of the Harem* (1873), became the basis for Margaret Landon's novelization, *Anna and the King of Siam* (1944), which in turn inspired a film of the same name with Irene Dunne and Rex

Harrison (1946); the Rodgers and Hammerstein musical (1951); the Deborah Kerr/Yul Brynner film, *The King and I* (1956); and most recently *Anna and the King* (1999), starring Jodie Foster and Chow Yun-Fat.[1] In each of these iterations of her story, Leonowens as governess is celebrated as a teacher of Western ideals of freedom to an Eastern despot and the martyred women of his court.

Leonowens fashioned *The English Governess* and two of her subsequent books—*The Romance of the Harem* and *Life and Travels in India* (1884)—as factual first-person narratives, part personal reminiscence, part reportage.[2] Leonowens's narrative voice does not claim the psychological verisimilitude of realist fiction that, for example, prompted G. H. Lewes to celebrate Charlotte Brontë as a novelist for the "reality—deep, significant reality" (691) with which she had imaginatively endowed Jane Eyre. Rather, Leonowens's narrator asserts both her veracity and her identity with the author, the witnessing Anna Leonowens.[3] In her preface to *The English Governess,* for example, Leonowens writes: "In the following pages I have tried to give a full and faithful account of the scenes and the characters that were gradually unfolded to me as I began to understand the [Siamese] language" (vii).[4] The "I" who makes this assertion is represented as continuous not only with the "I" who introduces the travelogue that follows ("I rose before the sun, and ran on deck to catch an early glimpse of the strange land we were nearing" [1]) but also with the "I" who will later parlay the success of *The English Governess* into a career as a writer, lecturer, and teacher.[5] Whether they find the governess protagonist an exemplar of English pluck or English imperialism, global feminist sisterhood or Western feminist arrogance, readers and revisers of Leonowens's narratives of heroic pedagogy have tended to accept her own apparent conflation of author and narrator.

In fact, as subsequent research has revealed, Leonowens's first-person narratives not only contain dubious assertions about the events and personalities they purport to describe, but also obscure as much as they reveal about Leonowens's own origins and the nature of her achievement—an obscurity she perpetuated not only in public versions of her story but also privately, to her family, whose beliefs about Leonowens's background were communicated to later biographers. Already, at her death, the *Montreal Star*'s admiring obituary misstated small but telling details. Leonowens's husband had not been *Major Leonowens,* but *Corporal* Thomas Leon *Owens;* her father had been a sergeant, not a captain; and available evidence suggests that she was born in India, not Wales. With a few alterations in proper names—the names proper to patrilineage and British imperialism—Leonowens rewrote her origins to match the social status that she later attained, erasing the actual labor of self-making.

As a self-made woman, Leonowens made shrewd use of the pedagogical roles available to an enterprising Victorian woman with a peripheral relationship to the urban centers of feminist educational reform in England—governess, author, expositor of foreign cultures. But as the author of her own story—a story that asserted her respectability, her Englishness, and her moral and pedagogical authority— she also drew upon the literary conventions that, as I have been arguing, characterize domestic fiction's representations of female intellectual ambition and pedagogical power. Like *Jane Eyre,* the governess story that precedes it by twenty-three years, *The English Governess* attempts the rhetorically complicated maneuver of narrating, in the first person, its protagonist's moral and intellectual ascendancy while dissociating her from the taint of illicit knowledge and experience; and like *Jane Eyre, The English Governess* is structured—although its tensions are not finally resolved—by the centrality of the heterosexual encounter and the marriage plot.[6]

Twentieth-century retellings have enthusiastically elaborated Leonowens's pursuit of innocence and heterosexual respectability. These retellings have not only produced an "Anna Leonowens" ever more dissociated from the contexts of class, gender, and nation that shaped Leonowens's pedagogical career, but they also have eliminated the complexities and conflicts that fracture Leonowens's own more polysemous combinations of memoir, travelogue, and novelistic convention. Caren Kaplan, one of Leonowens's recent readers from within feminist postcolonial criticism, remarks that "the celebrations of individualism, modernization, romance, and sisterhood that mark all the versions of Anna Leonowens's sojourn in Thailand are a crucial part of the reproduction of colonial discourse in modernity, including our supposedly 'postcolonial' moment" (35).[7]

If we focus on Leonowens's own texts, however, we can adopt Sara Mills's view of women's travel texts "in the colonial period as the site for many discursive conflicts: the writers were at one and the same time part of the colonial enterprise, and yet marginalised within it" (106). Mills is concerned with discourses of colonialism and femininity; to these "discursive pressures" (107) I would add conventions of genre. Attending to Leonowens's self-representation as a pedagogical woman who derives her authority from the capacity both to receive and to relay enlightenment, this chapter places her texts in conversation with two contemporary cultural scripts—the Western feminist ideal of the middle-class woman's pedagogic mission to non-Western women; and the literary conflict between trajectories of self-education and self-making, on the one hand, and the exclusive claim of the marriage plot to provide closure to the plots of *women's* self-making, on the other.

Leonowens's representation of herself as an intellectual and moral emissary to Siamese women is partly grounded in the nineteenth-century Orientalist and colonialist "Othering" assumptions of difference and inferiority that include backwardness at both the historical and the individual level (the culture is primitive or timeless; the people servile or childlike); religious inferiority; and mental and physical degradation.[8] The author not only of the Siam texts but also of *Life and Travels in India* (1884) and *Our Asiatic Cousins* (1889) (the only one of her books to include no first-person narrative),[9] Leonowens certainly placed herself within what Edward W. Said calls the "scientific discipline" of Orientalism, writing about countries that were, at that time, "important and politically urgent region[s] of the world" (206).[10] She asserts the veracity of her accounts both on her own authority as an eyewitness (*English Governess*, vii; *Romance of the Harem*, "Preface") and as an aspect of her place in a lineage of male-defined authority. In the preface to *The English Governess*, Leonowens not only associates herself with, but also asserts her predominance over, male, European experts: "Those of my readers who may find themselves interested in the wonderful ruins recently discovered in Cambodia are indebted to the earlier travelers, M. Henri Mouhot, Dr. A. Bastian, and the able English photographer, James Thomson, F. R. G. S. L., *almost as much* as myself" (vii; emphasis added). Throughout, her frequent recourse to a factual third-person voice makes no concession to her exclusion from the exclusively masculine institutions (universities and royal societies) understood to provide credentials for such assertions.

As Said points out, however, Orientalism as a professional field "was an exclusively male province."[11] Despite her alignment of herself with a male-identified Orientalist narrative voice, Leonowens remains peripheral to its authority, by virtue of what Susan Brown describes as "the ex-centricity of [her] position in terms not only of gender but also of class, racial, and national origin" (602). This "ex-centricity" has implications for both Leonowens's narrative choices and the reception of her texts and the authorial persona they imply. Within the texts, her reliance on Orientalist conventions varies sharply according to whether Leonowens is writing about Siamese men or Siamese women. In *The English Governess,* she often represents Siamese men as simultaneously sexually aggressive and effeminate: "I turned on [the premier's half brother] angrily, and bade him be off. The next moment this half-brother of a Siamese magnate was kneeling in abject supplication in the half-open doorway, imploring me not to report him to his Excellency . . . . Rage, cunning, insolence, servility, and hypocrisy were vilely mixed in the minion" (18). The half-brother represents an inassimilable and essential sensuality and corruption, to which the only appropriate response is repulsion. No educational exchange, or even patronage, is possible.

Contrarily, Leonowens generally represents Siamese women as heroically resistant to an unchristian and patriarchal society: "I was thankful to find, even in this citadel of Buddhism, men, and *above all women,* who were 'lovely in their lives.' . . . On the other hand, I have to confess with sorrow and shame, how far we, with all our boasted enlightenment, fall short, in true nobility and piety, of some of our 'benighted' sisters of the East"—(vii; emphasis added). Although the implication of the phrase "even in this citadel of Buddhism" is unmistakably denigrating, Leonowens nevertheless clearly asserts the "nobility and piety" of Siamese women, using quotation marks to distance herself from the evaluation of them as "benighted." (Although Leonowens begins this observation by recognizing virtue in women *and* men, by the end of the paragraph she is speaking only of "sisters.") The virtue of Siamese women, Leonowens's texts suggest, is that, unlike Siamese men, they can be assimilated to a pedagogical project. They can be represented as objects of Western instruction, occasions for the Western narrator's own learning, or exemplary figures in lessons directed at Western readers. As I will demonstrate, this distinction structures Leonowens's representations of Siamese men and women throughout her texts, particularly her depiction of the king, on the one hand, and the women of the harem, on the other. Said suggests that women in male-authored Orientalist texts "are usually the creatures of a male power-fantasy" (207). Leonowens's women are equally "creatures" of a "fantasy"—in this case, of female martyrdom; but they consistently challenge, although they rarely alter, patriarchal power.

Leonowens's status as an authoritative interpreter of Siamese culture, however, has been under attack since the publication of *The English Governess*.[12] Western scholars as well as Thai scholars and readers have vigorously objected to both the general outlines of Leonowens's portrayal of King Mongkut and many of the specific events she describes.[13] Mills, pointing to the frequency with which women's nineteenth-century travel writing encountered accusations of falsehood or exaggeration, argues that these accusations are rooted in assumptions about gender, including "a European cultural stereotype which casts women as duplicitous" and the fact that the agency of the female characters in women's travel writing appears "discursively anomalous" in contrast to women's more conventional portrayal in "literary and other texts . . . as passive objects, dependent on male characters" (115).

Leonowens's detractors do respond to her assertions of eyewitness authority and her pedagogical claims by attacking her on the grounds of her gender and class position.[14] A. B. Griswold, who accuses Leonowens of plagiarism, also calls her "emotionally unstable" (49); the descriptive copy on the back of the 1988 Oxford University reprint of *The English Governess* warns the reader that "like many Victorian ladies, [Leonowens] was always ready to expect the worst"; and Ian Grimble, the commentator in a 1970 documentary, describes her as "a squalid little girl, . . . one of those awful little English governesses, a sex-starved widow" (qtd. in *Romance of the Harem,* xi). Gender and class get Leonowens coming and going: she is too much a lady to be taken seriously for the author of the Oxford University Press copy, yet too little of a lady for Grimble.

On her own representation, Leonowens did share with her contemporaries a belief in the superiority and universal applicability of the norms of an individualist feminism inflected by both Victorian gender ideology, which valued women as exemplars of moral "purity," and Christian dogma. Leonowens's position, however, differed from that of better-known reformers, such as Mary Carpenter and Josephine Butler, who engaged in educational philanthropy on behalf of women of the colonies after long philanthropic careers on behalf of English women. Her motivations in coming to Siam derived neither, in the first instance, from a commitment to what Antoinette Burton identifies as "[English] feminists' quest to identify themselves and their cause with British national-imperial enthusiasm, politics, and glory" (35) nor from the ambitious restlessness that Barbara N. Ramusack finds among the five notable women she discusses to whom "India offered . . . opportunities for professional achievements or spiritual satisfaction" (128) as teachers and reformers.[15] Leonowens came reluctantly, out of financial desperation, to a country in which England had no colonial infrastructure in place to lend material weight to Orientalist attitudes. (Indeed, Leonowens seems to have been shunned, perhaps out of snobbery, by the English diplomatic community in Siam [Bristowe, 30–31].) She began writing *The English Governess* to make money after she left Siam in poor health; the inconsistency of representation and heterogeneity of style within and between *The English Governess* and *The Romance of the Harem* seem to be responses to her interpretation of audience requirements as well as to the "conflicting discursive pressures" (Mills, 106–7) of Orientalism, feminism, and feminine respectability.[16]

That inconsistency and heterogeneity is not negligible. *The English Governess* is predominantly a first-person narrative of events observed and participated in by Leonowens over the five-year period between her arrival at and departure from Siam. But its apparently autobiographical narrator offers little direct personal detail, and entire chapters of third-person narrative intervene to relate general cultural and historical details rather than immediate occurrences. *The Romance of the Harem,* despite a prefatory assertion that "[m]ost of the stories, incidents, and characters are known to me personally to be real," and the intermittent appearance of a witnessing and intervening "I," consists largely of interpolated tales told by or about Siamese women of a variety of castes and faiths. The representation of King Mongkut both within and across the two texts similarly does not conform to the expectations of narrative consistency common to both biography and realist fiction; in *The English Governess* he is alternately statesmanlike, ridiculous, and demonic; in *The Romance of the Harem,* which covers the same period of time, he is simply monstrous.

The narratives, in other words, are a *bricolage* of the styles and conventions of travelogue, memoir, domestic realism, and sensation fiction.

Nevertheless, as Margaret Landon revealed when she excised the historical material, grafted the sensational anecdotes in *The Romance of the Harem* on to the relatively more unified narrative spine of *The English Governess,* and recast the whole in the free indirect style of fictional realism, Leonowens's representation of her encounter with King Mongkut can be read according to the conventions of the courtship-and-marriage plot of the English domestic novel, and particularly its fantasy of the triumph of feminine (although not necessarily feminist) values over patriarchal values, embodied definitively for the nineteenth century in *Jane Eyre*.[17] In fact, it is this strand of Leonowens's story—the conventionally novelistic, tragicomic conflict between charismatic individuals of different sex and social standing—that has proven most enduringly popular for Western readers in the texts' transformations.

At the same time, however, the marriage plot that—however stressfully—resolves the tensions of *Jane Eyre* has the effect of multiplying tensions within *The English Governess.* This difference is partly the result of differing generic conventions. First, Leonowens's "I" may be as much a fictional character as Brontë's, but its authority depends on the reader's conviction of its autobiographical verisimilitude, as well as on the more easily verifiable accuracy of her statements about public figures such as King Mongkut: the reader therefore knows from the outset that no resolution of the narrative's conflicts by marriage between Leonowens and Mongkut will occur. Second, the conflicts between Rochester and Jane of status and moral and intellectual standing are contingent and temporary. The divisions in *The English Governess,* however—between Buddhism and Christianity, polygamy and monogamy, East and West—are represented as essential, all iterations of a fundamental conflict between ignorance and knowledge. Familiar and exuberantly reduplicative binary pairs of symbols—king/subject, man/woman, West/East, Christian/pagan—each of which signifies the same relation of power to subordination, become productive, rather than simply repetitive, because of their failure clearly to reassert that ontological pattern. "King," the symbol of national power, is in this narrative linked to "East," the geographical sign of national subjection, while "woman," the object of conquest, is linked to "West," the geographical sign of empire. *The English Governess* sorts these oppositions into two narrative axes: that of the confrontation between governess and king, and that of the encounter of the governess and the harem; but both trajectories are driven by an instability and vacillation that prevents either from leading to the safe harbor of the marriage plot.

Along the axis of the confrontation between governess and king, this instability is fundamentally elaborated by Leonowens's own contradictory accounts of the king's character and by her conflicting attitudes toward him. For example, having lived as a monk for many years before his accession to the throne, Mongkut, Leonowens says, is an ascetic and a scholar who has "habits of severe simplicity and frugality" and is "more systematically educated, and a more capacious devourer of books and news, than perhaps any man of equal rank in our day" (97). But she also represents the monkish scholar as a figure of fun, a marionette or a monkey. On her introduction to him, "His Majesty spied us quickly, and advanced abruptly, petulantly screaming, 'Who? who? who?'" (57). Like Jane Eyre when Rochester despotically commands her to converse, Leonowens resists the king's interrogation; as he continues to question her in a "high, sharp, key" he becomes, in her eyes, "indescribably comical" (59).[18] More damningly, Leonowens presents the king on later occasions as a demon of concupiscence. He imprisons and beats a lady of the harem for a trivial fault; in a severe transgression against the text's most valorized term—maternity—he punishes a mother who has gambled away her property by having her flogged in front of her heartbroken daughter. Yet she also subsequently shows him expressing, on the occasion of the death of his favorite daughter, Fâ-Ying, feelings that Leonowens admires as unimpeachably maternal: "Bitterly he bewailed his darling, calling her by such tender, touching epithets as the lips of loving Christian mothers use" (119).

Because of the narrative's peculiarly anecdotal structure—Fâ-Ying is both introduced and killed off in the chapter immediately following the flogging episode, without any narrative bridge—Leonowens does not fashion these successive impressions into a coherent character or represent them as participating in a consistent set of social norms. Regardless of the truth of any or all of these representations of a historical figure, indeed, they run the gamut of conflicting, if not self-canceling, Western representations of Eastern character: the ascetic and the demonic, the mysterious and the ludicrous, the patriarchal and the feminized—as though the fact that the king is "Oriental" obviates the need for consistency in representation. Indeed, Leonowens attributes the inconsistency to the culture itself, which she represents as "a troubled dream, delirious in contrast with the coherence and stability of Western life" (286), confused in its customs, beliefs, and impulses toward Westernization. At the same time, however, the instability of the king as a figure inevitably creates an instability in Leonowens's own self-representation, since she seems unable to make up her mind what the king signifies or how to evaluate him.

This instability is to some degree countered by the fact that Leonowens claims predominant pedagogical and scholarly authority in her text. This role, however, requires her to discount the king's reputation for erudition in many languages, including English, and many disciplines, including theology and astronomy. Her acknowledgments of the king's scholarship are always qualified, as when she writes that Mongkut "was more systematically educated, and a more capacious devourer of books and news, than perhaps any man of equal rank in our day. But much learning had made him morally mad; his extensive reading had engendered in his mind an extreme scepticism concerning all religious systems" (97). Leonowens elsewhere, however, joins the consensus of other historians of Mongkut's reign in calling him "toward priests, preachers, and teachers, of all creeds, sects, and sciences, an enlightened exemplar of tolerance" (56). These depictions again suggest an instability in Leonowens's view; they also undercut her claim to be the text's most powerful knowing subject.

According to historians, including Leonowens, the king's desire to have English education at his court, which brings Leonowens to Siam, was part of a diplomatic policy of openness designed to secure the country from Western colonization. From Mongkut's point of view, his interest in learning from the English is not a concession to the superiority of their culture, but, on the contrary, a sign of his own power and foresight. Negotiating Leonowens's hiring, the king reminds his employee that "We hope that in doing your education on us and on our children . . . you will do your best endeavor for knowledge of English language, science, and literature, and not for conversion to Christianity" (qtd. in *English Governess,* vi). Leonowens, however, proceeds from different assumptions, according to which she is less an employee than an emblem of superior morality, and she reads the king's distinction between proselytizing and pedagogy as a confrontation between error and truth. Thus his rejection of missionary intercession becomes the sign of a native incapacity and susceptibility to "the dazzle of the golden throne in the distance which arrested him midway between Christianity and Buddhism, between truth and delusion, between light and darkness, between life and death" (56).

Leonowens does not systematically evangelize, but she records with satisfaction her occasional successes: "Step by step," she writes, "I led [Fâ-Ying] out of the shadow-land of myth into the realm of the truth as it is in Christ Jesus" (117). Such a role is particularly compatible with the emphasis of English domestic ideology on women's responsibility for moral and religious superintendence of the family. But these displays of moral certitude conflict with Leonowens's equal insistence on her scholarly appreciation of Buddhism. She declares, for example, that "Many have missed seeing what is true and wise in the doctrine of Buddha because they preferred to observe it from the standpoint and in the attitude of an antagonist, rather than of an inquirer," and suggests adopting rather "the humble spirit of [a] fellowship of fallibility" (186). The scholarly and fallible "inquirer" and the bearer of absolute truth coexist uneasily. Leonowens neither fully inhabits the presumptively masculine scholarly role nor completely embraces the conventionally feminine power of moral influence. Furthermore, it is not clear why her display of ecumenicism is laudable, while the king's constitutes "moral madness," an ambiguity that again suggests an instability in Leonowens's self-representation and in the balance of power in the antagonistic relationship between herself and the king. This instability undermines, although it does not overcome, the text's dominant representation of Leonowens as the knower and Mongkut and Siam as the known.

Like the ideological contest between Leonowens and the king, their material conflict—over whether Leonowens will live within the harem, as the king wishes, or outside its walls, as she insists—ends in a draw. This conflict is the narrative's nightmare inversion of the marriage plot. The "Nang Harm," or harem, is an enclosed city of some nine thousand (by Leonowens's estimate) wives, concubines, and children of the king, many of them arriving as tribute from "noble[s], prince[s], and merchant[s] [seeking] to gain the royal favor by gifts thus presented" (*Romance,* 15). In Leonowens's depiction the Nang Harm is a burlesque of the idealized English home, blurring that space's strict boundaries between the political and the familial, the mercenary and the emotional, the "public woman," or prostitute, and the symbol of private life, the angel of the house. For Leonowens to live in the palace might challenge the distinction she strives to make between herself and the women of the harem, revealing an essential similarity between the position of king's concubine and that of English governess—both occupying the position of the *not-wife*, both dependent on patriarchal pleasure, both not, from the perspective of domestic ideology, at home.

Leonowens resists naming this danger. Asked by the king why she will not sleep in the palace, "'I do not clearly know,' I replied, with a secret shudder at the idea of sleeping within those walls; 'but I am afraid I could not do it'" (65). Leonowens's "secret shudder," a tremor that can suggest pleasure as easily as horror, reveals her contamination by precisely the knowledge of the sexual from which she is attempting to protect herself. The king's question, "Where do you go every evening?" betrays a distrust of female mobility that is not peculiar to the Siamese harem—governesses in England also were not expected to leave the family home alone after dark. Feminist texts of the period, public and private, often allude to the imprisoning possibilities of domestic bliss: "It is considered a just cause for surprise and disappointment," writes Emily Davies in *The Higher Education of Women,*

> that well brought up girls, surrounded with all the comforts
> of home, should have a wish or a thought extending beyond
> its precincts. And, perhaps, it is only natural that parents
> should be slow to encourage their daughters in aspirations
> after any duties and interests besides those of ministering to
> their comfort and pleasure. In taking it for granted that this
> is the only object, other than that of marriage, for which
> women were created, they are but adopting the received sen-
> timent of society. (50–51)

Davies makes no explicit analogy with the harem, but the picture of women contained within the "precincts" of the home, their only duties the provision of "comfort and pleasure," is pointed.[19]

Not surprisingly, then, the search for a suitable home exposes Leonowens to indignity and sexual threat, as the king first leaves her to languish for several months in the palace of the Kralahome (the premier of the kingdom) and then offers her a residence she considers unsuitable, a filthy apartment in a fish market. Fleeing this insult to herself in both domestic and professional characters, Leonowens is "stopped by a crowd of men, women, and children, half naked, who gathered around me, wondering. . . . I was glad to accept the protection of my insulted escort [the king's messenger], and escape from that suburb of disgust" (69). The adventure prostrates Leonowens with fever for almost a week, during which she is "tortured day and night with frightful fancies and dreams" (70) whose content goes unspecified. The next house with which she is presented has "pleasant and airy" rooms, although they are covered with "filthy filth, so monstrous in quantity and kind" (74)—filth whose exact nature, like the content of Leonowens's febrile dreams, goes unrevealed. It is difficult, however, not to associate the "fancies," "dreams," and "monstrous" filth with the sexual threat that, in her view, the harem poses. Notably, that threat is produced (as "dreams" and "fancies") within Leonowens's own consciousness as well as besmirching her from without, just as her flight from the palace can be read as revealing the very sexual knowledge from which she seeks to distance herself.

In this second instance, however, Leonowens triumphs, in a scene of purification that invokes every symbol of English domesticity—cleanliness, prayer, cooking, maternity: "Suddenly I arose . . . marched through a broken door, hung my hat and mantle on a rusty nail, doffed my neat half-mourning, slipped on an old wrapper, dashed at the vile matting that in ulcerous patches afflicted the floor, and began fiercely tearing it up. . . . How quickly the general foulness was purified, the general raggedness repaired, the general shabbiness made 'good as new'!" (75). Having dispatched the apartment's native filth, Leonowens paints an English domestic still life of silver candlesticks, books, piano, tea. The presence of servants ("Then came comfortable Beebe with the soup and dainties she had prepared") and even a defunct husband glanced at in the reference to Leonowens's mourning dress complete the legitimacy of the domestic ménage. Finally Leonowens puts her son to sleep: "Triumphantly I bore him to his own pretty couch, adjusted my hair, resumed my royal robes of mauve muslin, and prepared to queen it in my own palace" (76)—one of Leonowens's rather infrequent invocations of her maternity.[20]

Leonowens's is the definitively English "palace" of Victoria, the devoted wife who is the antitype not only of the polygamous king but also of the king's queens and concubines.[21] Leonowens's representation of her domestic triumph, however, has less comforting undercurrents. First, unlike her contest with the king over claims to scholarly and pedagogical authority, winning the battle over Leonowens's location—actual (palace or private home) and symbolic (sexualized female dependent or disembodied professional woman)—depends not on her pedagogical power but on her ability to imitate, if not to incarnate, the angelic housewife of domestic ideology. Second, the chapter ends not with Leonowens's tantric recital of household gods—"Beebe, soup, teapot, candlesticks, teacups, and dear faithful Bessy [the dog], looked on and smiled" (76)—but with the king's summons to the schoolroom, where the symbols of English womanhood are once again subject to indignity. "[The young women students] . . . donned my hat and cloak, and made a promenade of the pavilion; another pounced upon my gloves and veil, and disguised herself in them, to the great delight of the little ones" (86). The chapter reveals the tenuousness with which Leonowens inhabits the persona of either the professional or the domestic English woman.

Despite such moments of fracture, *The English Governess,* like other texts informed by domestic ideology (such as Harriet Beecher Stowe's *Uncle Tom's Cabin,* which Leonowens admired), is structured by a fantasy of power in which women's teaching rearranges social structures to produce the triumph of feminine values as well as the advancement of the individual woman. According to Leonowens's account, her combative behavior finally brings her a position of respect at the court: she is called upon by the king for help with English language and customs and by the women for her intercessory powers. With this respect comes social advancement. King Mongkut, in a letter she reprints, addresses her as "Lady Leonowens," a title to which, in her own country, she has no claim, and confers on her an honorary "title of nobility" and a matching estate. Different conventions of gender in language create the appearance of having achieved mobility not only of class, but also of gender, as Leonowens finds herself frequently addressed as "sir" by such dignitaries as the premier's sister and the premier himself.[22] If such usages are effects of linguistic difference they nevertheless emphasize, in Leonowens's English text, that the power she appears to have attained depends not only on social rank but also on gender.

But even as it is enacted, the fantasy of mobility reveals itself as only fantasy, dependent on linguistic misinterpretation and therefore significant only in her textual re-creation. The national power encrypted in her gender and class transformations signifies as such only paradoxically when Leonowens leaves home: that is, it is only because she is an English woman *abroad* that the "fact" of her nationality brings her recognition. And yet to be abroad is never to be recognized. The premier's sister's "Good morning, sir," represents the only English she knows; the goodwill it expresses is formal, not informed, for she will use it "though the hour were night" (61). And Leonowens never takes possession of the estate bestowed upon her, which can be reached only by a long journey by elephant through the jungle. Finally, the national power that Leonowens imagines herself to represent is itself far from absolute. A trivial diplomatic quarrel contributes to the decline of her position at court and to her departure.

The finality of even this anticlimactic end to Leonowens's sojourn is itself formally undermined. True, Leonowens asserts that the king "who had been silent and sullen until the morning of my departure, relented when the time came to say goodbye"; he tells her that she is "much beloved by our common people, and all inhabitants of palace and royal children. . . . It shall be because you must be a good and true lady" (283). And the departing Leonowens is waved on by "all our European friends" (285). The status of "a good and true lady" blessed with "European friends" is what the narrative has aimed to confer upon its narrator, but it cannot quite erase the textual traces of Leonowens's financial insecurity, obscure past, and uncertain future—in the terms of English society, she remains only dubiously "good," "true," or "a lady."

Furthermore, the valedictory tone achieved here is blunted by the fact that this chapter—"My Retirement from the Palace"—is followed by three more, all impersonal third-person travelogue. As a result, the last words of the memoir turn entirely from the West, appearing to celebrate the religion that Leonowens has earlier described as Christianity's "shadow": "And [Prince Somannass] caused the face of the great P'hra Indara to be carved on the north and on the south and on the east and on the west [of the temple]—so that all men might know the true God, who is God alone in heaven, Sevarg-Savan!" (321). Certainly these chapters celebrate Leonowens's achievement insofar as they demonstrate for the reader her mastery of Orientalist knowledge. But the replacement of governess by scholar remains incomplete: a vacillating but lively first-person narrative and a stiff third-person exposition remain unblended and mutually vexing in *The English Governess,* and the book finally presents its narrator as triumphant over neither the constrictions of her own culture, nor the traditions of the Siamese culture. Leonowens's great success story—her manipulation of her own experiences in the margins of imperial culture to re-create herself as an enlightened Lady Bountiful—cannot, as a *condition* of its success, be written.

The meaning and power of feminine influence and pedagogy is also at stake in the competing narrative strand of *The English Governess,* Leonowens's encounter with the women of the harem. When Leonowens wearies of her duties to the king—"translating, correcting, copying, dictating, reading"—she finds it a "consolation to know that I could befriend the women and children of the palace. . . . With no intention on my part, and almost without my own consent, I suffered myself to be set up between the oppressor and the oppressed. From that time I had no peace" (270). From "consolation" to "no peace": like her attitude toward the king, Leonowens's relationship to the women of the harem vacillates, as she asserts a cross-cultural sisterhood that succeeds only partially in repositioning the economically vulnerable barracks widow as the educated, influential Western intercessor.

Just as Leonowens's representations of the king and his culture draw on Orientalist assumptions and novelistic plot conventions of heterosexual pairing, her representation of the women of the Nang Harm draws both on contemporary feminist representations of Eastern, non-Christian women as sexually victimized and enslaved and on the narrative conventions of hagiography—the telling of the saint's or martyr's life which, for women, offers one of the few narrative alternatives to courtship and marriage. As the figure of the female pedagogue became more visible in late-Victorian culture, beginning in the 1860s, she began to share the stage with an apparently completely different kind of female figure: the sexually exploited woman. Victorian feminist activism was often structured by hierarchical relations of contrast between the two figures, as well as assertions of sisterhood. Josephine Butler, for example, was involved in the English education campaigns in the 1860s and also led the movement to repeal the Contagious Diseases Acts (1869–86), which subjected women suspected of prostitution in port and garrison towns in England to medical detention. She later promoted women's education in India and opposed the extension of the Contagious Diseases Acts there (Burton, 130–40). As Antoinette Burton argues, "The move [for Butler] from 'home' to India and from working-class women to Indian womanhood was facilitated by the dependent posture in which British feminists imagined both their domestic and their colonial female clienteles" (143). Whether in England or abroad, along axes of nation or class, the sexually victimized woman in the 1860s and 1870s was being re-created by English feminist activism as the "sister" of the sexually unmarked woman—but always the younger, untutored, sister, whose straits justified the activities and energies of the elder.

In English women's travel writing, the sequestered Eastern or Middle Eastern woman served similarly as a foil for self-representation. Leila Ahmed describes a Western male Orientalist tradition of representing the harem that focused on "women being freely and continuously together, and the degradation, licentiousness, and corruption that must inevitably ensue," and included "prurient speculation . . . about women's sexual relations with each other within the harem" (524).[23] Victorian feminist writers eschewed such "prurient speculation" in favor of representing harem women—like working-class prostitutes or women under slavery, with whom they were emblematically conjoined —as victims of, not collaborators in, patriarchal sexual license. For Leonowens, the women of the harem, living under the double indentures of concubinage and bond slavery, are "ill-fated sisters of mine, imprisoned without a crime! . . . The misery which checks the pulse and thrills the heart with pity in one's common walks about the great cities of Europe is hardly so saddening as the nameless, mocking wretchedness of these women, to whom poverty were a luxury, and houselessness as a draught of pure, free air" (*English Governess,* 104). This "wretchedness" becomes the basis for a narrative of martyrdom.

Although Leonowens's rhetoric and her activities on behalf of the women assert their sisterhood, her textual relationship to them is most frequently one of opposition. "These women" are unlike Leonowens not only in being enslaved, while she is free, but also in being parasitic, while she is productive. Leonowens often presents harem women as giggling, chattering, and inconsequent. Faced, on her arrival, with the women of the premier's harem *en masse,* she writes with apparent exasperation: "To be free to make a stunning din is a Siamese woman's idea of perfect enjoyment" (*English Governess,* 18). In response to their vocal curiosity, she asserts: "I am not like you. You have nothing to do but to play and sing and dance for your master; but I have to work for my children" (21–22). When Leonowens, having waited several months for an audience with the king, has "desperately settled down to my Oriental studies," the premier neatly underlines this opposition, observing, "Siamese lady no like work; love play, love sleep. Why you no love play?" (71).[24] The apparent absence of productive labor or intellectual activity on the part of the women of the harem distinguishes them from the English woman who earns her living through her intellectual labor.

But the negative representation of the harem women's "play" suppresses less authorizing readings of the distinction between productive and unproductive women. The leisure of the women of the harem whom Leonowens encounters is in fact a sign of a class status higher than that of the English governess, whose labor in her own culture is undervalued when it does not actually threaten loss of caste. In the same year that Leonowens was diligently applying herself to her "Oriental studies," the *Quarterly Review* continued to insist that "the duties of women do not to any great extent lie in the intellectual direction" ("Female Education," 465) and that if (as the article concedes) women must be trained as governesses, the aim should be not professional expertise or intellectual cultivation but the acquirements of an upper domestic servant: "simplicity of living, the strictest economy . . . training in housekeeping, regular needlework, and, if possible, actual schoolteaching" (467–68). The opposition that Leonowens draws between the woman of the harem and the female educator can be read, then, less as an attempt to comprehend and represent the lives and activities of Siamese women than as an example of the attempt of Victorian feminism to reconstitute women's economic or intellectual productivity, by contrasting it with a sensual indolence, as virtuous rather than suspect.

Moving beyond Leonowens's own representation, the gap between her likely background, as re-created by Bristowe and Dow, and her implicit reconstruction of it suggests another possible displacement in her insistence on the victimization of the harem women. Bristowe cites a description of the lives of the wives of enlisted soldiers (such as Leonowens's mother) in India:

Mrs. Postum paints a terrible picture in the year 1838: "Unable, from extreme heat, to move out of the little room allotted to them in the married men's quarters during the day, and provided for two rupees a month with a Portuguese 'cook boy' who relieves them from the toil of domestic duties, the only resource of the soldiers' wives is in mischievous associations, discontented murmurings, and habits of dissipated indulgence." (27–28)

The similarities in this account to representations of the harem—immurement, indolence, unspecified forms of "indulgence"—are clear. Dow's equally speculative account of Leonowens's childhood emphasizes, not the indolence, but the hard sexual and domestic labor that wives and daughters of enlisted men performed: "Soldiers' wives had to be more than equal to the tough lives they had chosen. They were encouraged to supplement their husbands' meager wages by doing the regiment's wash, and a bride was often chosen for her hardiness as much as anything else" (3). According to Dow, the family would have lost their entitlement to army rations and accommodation within a year after the death of Anna's father; Leonowens's mother remarried just three months after giving birth to Anna. Leonowens's sister, Eliza, was married at the age of fourteen to a thirty-eight-year-old sergeant-major (2, 4). Despite their different emphases, both Bristowe's and Dow's accounts point up the sexual and economic dependency that characterized the lives of camp followers and enlisted men's wives and daughters.

In this light, Leonowens's horror at the sight of the harem, and her representation of herself as an intercessor for the harem women, can be read as demonstrating not her freedom from sexual contamination and her agency, but her determination to *reconstruct* herself as an uncontaminated agent. It is possible that Leonowens felt a kinship with some of the women she met grounded in analogous experience. Her narrative, however, largely represents her sororal relations with the women of the harem as intercessions from a world beyond them:

> Whenever the king should be dangerously enraged, and
> ready to let loose upon some tender culprit of the harem the
> monstrous lash or chain, I—at a secret cue from the head

wife—was to enter upon his Majesty, book in hand, to consult his infallibility in a pressing predicament of translation into Sanskrit, Siamese, or English. . . . Under cover of this naïve device from time to time a hapless girl escaped the fatal burst of his wrath. (276)

The scene represents a collaboration between Leonowens and the "head wife," Lady Thieng, but it also draws a sharp distinction between the easily duped king and his "hapless" girls, on the one hand, and the cunning and mobile Leonowens, on the other.

At the same time, however, Leonowens's representation of herself as a powerful intercessor is undercut not only by the failures of her intercessory power but also, intermittently, by an alternative interpretation of the filiations of the harem, an institution that, Ahmed has suggested, can be viewed not only as a patriarchal disposal of women but also as "a system" that "enables women to have frequent and easy access to other women in their community, vertically, across class lines, as well as horizontally" (524). Leonowens's representation of the harem frequently, if sensationally, supports such a reading: If the Nang Harm is a women's prison, it is also world in which women function productively and in support of each other. "This women's city," Leonowens writes, in *The Romance of the Harem,* "is as self-supporting as any other in the world: it has its own laws, its judges, police, guards, prisons, and executioners, its markets, merchants, brokers, teachers, and mechanics of every kind and degree; and every function of every nature is exercised by women, and by them only" (13). Leonowens's descriptions of harem life illustrate solidarity among women across class and generation. When the king, on the basis of "a stupid grudge" (*English Governess,* 108) orders one woman beaten, "the stripes were administered so tenderly, that the only confession they extorted was the meek protestation that she was 'his meanest slave, and ready to give her life for his pleasure'" (109); in a footnote, Leonowens adds, "In these cases the executioners are women, who generally spare each other if they dare."

Another anecdote in the same chapter demonstrates the mutual devotion of Wanne, Leonowens's, young pupil, who "learned to spell, read, and translate almost intuitively" (112); Wanne's loyal slave, Mai Noie, who "shared her scholarly enthusiasm" so that "all that Wanne learned at school in the day was lovingly taught to Mai Noie in the nursery at night" (113); and Wanne's profligate mother, in disgrace with the king for gambling. When the mother gambles away Mai Noie, the king orders her beaten. Wanne flings herself protectively across her mother's back. "There," writes Leonowens, "was a case for prayer. . . . Who could behold so many women crouching, shuddering, stupefied, dismayed, in silence and darkness, animated, enlightened only by the deep whispering heart of maternity, and not be moved with mournful yearning?" (115). Despite Leonowens's rhetorical question, neither the daughter's plea nor Leonowens's own presence prevents the sentence from being carried out. Leonowens here invokes the rhetorical function of maternity within Victorian domestic ideology as the distinctive, unifying, and uniformly valorized feature of womanhood. Insisting on the transcultural moral significance of "the deep whispering heart of maternity," however, requires Leonowens to ignore the specific diplomatic and cultural context of the Siamese court as she has elsewhere represented it. In that context, motherhood is part of an extended political and economic network of kinship relations quite different from the organization of the nineteenth-century English family, in either its ideal or its actual incarnations. What Leonowens represents here is not whatever role maternity may in fact have played in nineteenth-century Siamese gender ideology, but a scene of martyrdom rendered legible to her readers within overlapping conventions of Victorian domestic ideology and Victorian feminism.

These tales of the harem as a city of slavery, torture, and ecstatic martyrdom, along with the even more sensational stories in *The Romance of the Harem*, end up testifying to the mutual devotion and resistance of the harem women and to the powerlessness that Leonowens shares with them. Yet, of course, her assumption of the role of narrator reverses that shared powerlessness: hers is the power of representation. Leonowens's tales, Susan Morgan asserts in her introduction to *The Romance of the Harem,* "speak for the women of the harem as no other writing about Nang Harm has" (xxxvii). But it is precisely this act of "speaking for" that affirms a relation of opposition between Leonowens and the women of the harem. She is the teller, they are what is told; she is the interpreter, they are the raw material for Leonowens's indictment of a particular manifestation of patriarchal power. Leonowens's assertion that for "these women . . . poverty were a luxury, and houselessness as a draught of pure, free air" represents, as far as the reader can know, not their analysis of their circumstances, but her insistence on the difference of her own.

The English Governess as a narrative, then, remains marked by a tension between opposition and sorority and by Leonowens's conflicting attitudes toward her own agency, the king's power, and the power of female martyrdom. Like Leonowens herself, the heroines in her martyrs' gallery evade the dominant end of female desire in nineteenth-century fiction—marriage. But even more than Leonowens herself, they pay a high price for that evasion. I have suggested that Leonowens's narrative of her own achievement depends as much on self-censorship as on self advertisement—on silence about, or rewriting of, kinds of experience, pedagogy, and desire not recognized as part of the respectable woman's *Bildung*. Her narrative of Siamese women's heroism, similarly, and more thoroughly, depends on silencing as well as expression. Within the tales, women who speak out against their circumstances are frequently silenced by death or maiming. For example, the story of Wanne and her mother ends when, after Wanne's futile attempt to protect her, "the lash descended . . . *unforbidden by any cry*" (115; emphasis added). Literalizing the dangers of speech, one tale in *The Romance of the Harem* concludes with a slave woman cutting out her own tongue in order not to betray the flight from the palace of her mistress. Leonowens also censors the women's tales in the very act of giving them words, not only in the inevitable sense that she speaks for them, but also in the sense that the voices she includes are predominantly those that conform to the narrative structure she has chosen—that of martyrdom.[25]

Leonowens does provide alternative glimpses of apparently learned and effective women, such as her "interesting pupil, the Lady Talap" (*English Governess,* 186), who invites her to religious services that Leonowens then explicates for the reader; Khoon Thow App, a female magistrate of the court, "religious and scrupulously just" with "a serious and concentrated bearing" (59); and Sonn Klean, or "Hidden Perfume," who disputes with Leonowens the merits of Buddhist versus Christian forms of worship and who shares Leonowens's admiration for *Uncle Tom's Cabin* and frees her own slaves in tribute to Stowe

(*Romance of the Harem*, 248–50). As Leonowens relates in *The Romance of the Harem,* to be a member of the royal harem was to be highly educated: "In every ducal or royal harem there are a great many buildings designed and built for the express purpose of training and educating the women. . . . The female teachers, physicians, and judges, who are placed over them, generally receive a careful professional education,— the best the country can supply" (109). But the life histories that might have been shaped by a "careful professional education"—something then unavailable to any British woman—are visible only as fragments within Leonowens's narratives.

Both full control of her narrative and material power in the court may escape Leonowens in her Siam memoirs; but pedagogical power remains in her hands. The memoirs are demonstrations of her own capacity both to turn experience into knowledge and to instruct others— the women and children of the harem, and the readers of her books. At the same time, the Orientalist knowledge on display in the memoirs works to efface the traces of less legitimating kinds of experience and knowledge that might have been part of Leonowens's own *Bildung.* It also compensates for the unavailability of the conclusion that would resolve the emblematic differences between Leonowens and Mongkut decisively in favor of the woman and the values she represents: "Reader, I married him," in Jane Eyre's somberly triumphant words, as she leads the maimed, blinded, and reformed Rochester back into the domestic fold. But if this governess cannot be transformed into a scholar, neither can she be recuperated as a wife: the only available position at the king's court is that of concubine. ("Enormous sums were offered, year after year," according to Leonowens, "for an English woman of beauty and good parentage to crown the collection" [94].) The marriage plot fails Leonowens, even as it hovers tantalizingly above her tale, and fictional and social convention offer her no alternative realizable in narrative.

Despite the fractures in this pedagogical performance—both within the narrative, in its vacillating relations to its "others," and extratextually, in its uncertain relation to historical and biographical fact—readers have often been eager to embrace the fantasy of a feminine pedagogy powerful enough to affect the fate of a nation.[26] Reading *The English Governess* can provide a reminder of the multiple erasures on which such a fantasy depends—first, Leonowens's omission of narratively and ideologically inassimilable aspects of her own life history; second, the narrowing of representational possibility in her depiction of Siamese women as, largely, victims and martyrs; and finally, the elimination by later revisers of Leonowens of the traces of instability, conflict, and misunderstanding that mark the narrative's ambivalent relationship to its own fantasy of pedagogical power.

Chapter 4

"At once narrow and promiscuous"
Emily Davies, George Eliot, and *Middlemarch*

George Eliot began work on *Middlemarch* in 1869, in the same year that Girton College, Cambridge, opened its doors as the first institution of postsecondary education for women in England.[1] It is easy to imagine Eliot's "ardent, theoretic, and intellectually consequent" (24) heroine, Dorothea Brooke, among its five pioneering students; easier than many of her readers have found it to imagine her ultimate marriage to the dilettantish and facile Will Ladislaw. The relief of one of Girton's first students, Constance Maynard, "in the glorious conviction that at last, *at last* we were afloat on a stream that had a real destination" (qtd. in Vicinus, 137), captures the longing for direction that drives Dorothea into marriage with the pedantic exegete, Casaubon. She imagines that marriage as the highest sort of higher education: "The union which attracted her was one that would deliver her from her girlish subjection to her own ignorance, and give her the freedom of voluntary submission to a guide who would take her along the grandest path. . . . It would be like marrying Pascal. I should learn to see the truth by the same light as great men have seen it. And then I should know what to do, when I got older: I should see how it was possible to lead a grand life here—now— in England" (24).

In Dorothea's fantasized progression from "subjection" to "voluntary submission" to "lead[ing] a grand life," the ambition that flares intermittently beneath her Evangelical and philanthropic sacrifices makes itself felt. Eliot's devotion to the theme of renunciation, combined with the conventions of the *Bildungsroman,* make certain that the progress of the narrative will severely test and revise Dorothea's early understanding of the form and goal of her own higher education. In that sense alone, the topic of education is central to *Middlemarch.*

In addition to this centrality of education in the broadest sense, however—as the development of the individual in his or her social reality —*Middlemarch* is clearly a critique of education in a more specifically intellectual and institutional sense. Its characters' misunderstandings and tragedies are largely produced by failures of knowledge systems (the dilettante liberal education of Mr. Brooke; the exhausted exegetical tradition followed by Casaubon); delusions about the power conferred by knowledge as such (Lydgate's belief that medical studies have made him, and Dorothea's that classical studies will make her, wise); and the commodification of educational institutions (the *arriviste* training of Fred and Rosamond Vincy).[2] Further, within this theme of delusion uncorrected by knowledge, the novel's three central women, Dorothea Brooke, Rosamond Vincy, and Mary Garth, emerge as a middle-class triumvirate (with Dorothea at the apex) whose fates, taken individually and together, can be read as responses to the plans for women's higher education that Eliot's reforming feminist friends, such as Barbara Bodichon and Emily Davies, were beginning to instigate in the 1860s.

Indeed, during the time that Eliot was conceiving and publishing *Middlemarch* in serial installments, "the air [was] thick" as the *Quarterly Review* put it in 1869, "with plans for female education" ("Female Education," 448). Not only was Eliot involved with those schemes through her friendship with Bodichon, who worked with Davies on the foundation of Hitchin, and her subscription to the *English Woman's Journal,* but she also gave money for the foundation and books to the library (Haight, 460, Stephen, 227) and advised Davies on the proposed curriculum. The two questions addressed here, therefore, are: what precisely does Eliot, the most famous woman intellectual and "aesthetic teacher" of the period, understand to be the aim of education, and how does that understanding respond to the relative explosion of plans for the higher education of women contemporary with the period of *Middlemarch*'s composition?

By setting *Middlemarch* in the years immediately preceding the Reform Bill of 1832, Eliot makes Maynard's choice unavailable to Dorothea and renders the changes in women's education less obviously a topic of the novel.[3] Gillian Beer has suggested that "George Eliot uses the pivot of the unwritten years in *Middlemarch*—the years between setting and composition—to register some changes in women's circumstances, but rather small change in the actual conditions of women's lives. One of the sad speculative movements of the book is to bring into question the extent to which any real enfranchisement has been achieved between 1830 and 1870" (170). But the feminist reader of the 1870s, or even the casual reader of the quarterly journals, might well feel that certain conditions—particularly, institutional conditions—*had* changed; and Eliot herself was in the best position to be aware of those changes. Indeed, *Middlemarch*'s melancholia, irony, and evasive responses to the topic of women's education, I will argue, constitute Eliot's response to those changes. In addition to her conservative distrust of the ambition for public power demonstrated by political action, Eliot questions the effects of institutionalized knowledge systems, suggesting that they are easily commodified and rendered mediocre. She also questions the effect on the individual, and particularly the individual woman, of corporate actions and aims.

Eliot takes moral development to be at the heart of the educational project. She shares this concern with contemporary cultural and political theorists such as Matthew Arnold and John Stuart Mill, although her response is different. The two men, despite their political variance, both expected educational institutions to combat what they identified as the growing commodification and mental mediocrity of middle-class society. Eliot, on the other hand, identifies the broadening of institutional education, at least as it is currently constituted, as part of the problem. This skepticism also distinguishes her from the circle of intellectual women that included Davies and Bodichon, as she doubts that the incursion of women into these commodified institutions will increase their access to either self-fulfillment or moral wisdom. Arnoldian humanists, who ignored women's education *per se,* and feminist reformers, for whom it was the basis of women's condition, shared a liberal belief in education: they believed that revived, regularized institutions devoted to education would do much to bring, in Eliot's words, "the outer life of man . . . into harmony with his inward needs" (*Selected Essays*, 365). Eliot, however, doubted the power of institutions—even educational institutions—to effect this harmony. She celebrates in her most socially effective heroines (Romola, Dinah, Dorothea) their exclusion from institutions of cultural influence, as a kind of purity, and the compensation that she supplies is nostalgic—the reward of martyrdom.

When Davies, in the late 1860s, conceived the plan for a college for women, it was natural that their mutual friend Bodichon would encourage her to consult George Eliot, the most prominent intellectual woman of the period. The correspondence between Davies and Eliot on the topic of women's education makes particularly legible the tension between the pragmatic, if sometimes disguised, desire for participation in the public sphere that formed one aspect of the educational reform movement, and Eliot's more ambivalent and more idealized vision of education as the basis of self-mastery. Davies, as I have discussed in chapter 1, exemplifies the movement's concern with professional and institutional power, rather than primarily moral or intellectual gains. Although, as I have argued, she retains an ambivalent attachment to the modes of self-presentation prescribed for women by domestic ideology, and a suspicion of the rights-based language of liberal individualism, her denial of difference between women and men in the sphere of intellect, her emphasis on the self-determination of women as students, and the high value she places on action in the public sphere reveal the influence of liberal individualism. Because Eliot's relationship to liberal individualism was ambivalent, combining a concern with individuals at intellectual and emotional odds with their social situations (such as Maggie Tulliver and Dorothea Brooke) with an emphatic sense of the importance of social interrelations, her ambivalence about the project of transferring individualist values to women is not surprising. "I care so much about individual happiness that I think it is a great thing to work for, only to make half-a-dozen lives rather better than they might otherwise be," she wrote to Davies on the occasion of the college's opening (qtd. in Stephen, 227). In another letter to Davies, she called women's education "a great campaign [that] has to be victualled for"; and to Bodichon, she declared that "the better education of Women is one of the objects about which I have no doubt" (qtd. in Stephen, 170).

Nevertheless, the hesitant quality of her actual support has often been noted by feminist scholars.[4] For Eliot, the vocabulary of moral reconciliation was not merely strategic, and she objected on at least one occasion to Davies's nonchalance. "I have it on my conscience," she wrote to her, "that I did not make a little protest against something that fell from you about 'the family' and also about the hurrying industrial view of life that infects us all in these days" (qtd. in Stephen, 182). In a letter recounting one much later interview with Eliot, apropos of a course on morals that Davies's friend Adelaide Manning proposed to teach to secondary schoolgirls, Davies supplies an equivocal glimpse of the "view of life" that Eliot found more compelling:

> She hoped my friend would teach the girls not to think too much of political measures for improving society—as leading away from individual efforts to be good, I understood her to mean. I said I thought there was not much danger of that with girls. It is so much more inculcated upon them to be good and amiable than anything else. She said, was there not a great deal among girls of wanting to do some great thing and thinking it not worth while to do anything because they cannot do that? I said there might be, but I had not come across it. What I had met with more was not caring to do anything. She said, Yes, no doubt stupidity prevails more than anything. [. . .] At this stupidity stage I thought I had staid long enough and came away promising to try to remember to tell my friend what she had said. . . . It will be of great interest to her to have so much advice from such an authority. (Qtd. in Stephen, 185–86)

Despite her declared "reverence" for Eliot, Davies, many of whose friends and colleagues were schoolmistresses, might well have been tempted to reflect upon how few girls the socially tabooed author was likely to have come in contact with. Davies's account suggests a polite insistence on her own empirical observations (what she has "come across" and "met with") in the face of Eliot's hypothetical fears of moral stupidity. It is impossible to be sure whether her comment that "[i]t will be of great interest to [Manning] to have so much advice from such an authority" is sardonically or seriously intended.[5] The remark trades, consciously or not, on the paradox that while "George Eliot," the author, *was* considered an authority on morals, "Mrs. Lewes," the unmarried companion of G. H. Lewes, was considered an immoral woman, and Davies herself had wondered about the propriety of calling on her. Davies's letter both summarizes the difference between her views and Eliot's of the dangers of education and displays her typical equivocation in the face of traditional expectations of female morality.

Eliot's fears and expectations might seem to be fully addressed by the rather different educational program set forth in John Ruskin's popular testament to the angelic ideal rampant—"Of Queens' Gardens," whose aim has been characterized as being "to get comfortable middle-class women to leave their park walls and garden gates for a world of wilderness and secrets and suffering" (Helsinger, Sheets, and Veeder, 1:90). In this lecture, Ruskin describes at some length the appropriate education for one of his domestic "queens." In its moral content, he argues, "A girl's education [should] be as serious as a boy's. . . . Give them the same advantages that you give their brothers; appeal to the same grand instincts of virtue in them; teach them, also, that courage and truth are the pillars of their being" (Ruskin, 132). More overtly than Davies, and more cheerfully than Eliot, Ruskin acknowledges the existence of a female desire for power, which he believes can be brought into the service of the angelic vision: "Vainly, as falsely, you blame or rebuke the desire of power! For Heaven's sake, and for Man's sake, desire it all you can. But what power? . . . Power to heal, to redeem, to guide, and to guard; power of the sceptre and shield. . . . Will you not covet such power as this, and seek such throne as this, and be no more housewives, but queens?" (137).

But if Ruskin allows women the "power to heal, to redeem, to guide, and to guard," he explicitly rejects independent intellectual power as a goal for them. Ruskin advocated the kind of separate-and-unequal training that alarmed Davies in many schemes for women's university education. Women's knowledge was to be relative to men's needs: "All such knowledge should be given her as may enable her to understand, and even to aid, the work of men; and yet it should be given, not as knowledge,—not as if it were, or could be, for her, an object to know, but only to feel, and to judge" (125); and "a woman ought to know [a] language or science only so far as may enable her to sympathize in her husband's pleasures, and in those of his best friends" (128). Finally, girls are to receive this training osmotically and in solitude, rather than within an institution or as a corporate project: "Turn her loose into the old library every day, and let her alone. . . . You may chisel a boy into shape, as you would a rock . . . but you cannot hammer a girl into anything. . . . She must take her own fair form and way if she take any" (130–31).

Many of the ideas of this program—the emphasis on moral, rather than strictly intellectual, development; the concern with service rather than self-fulfillment; and the celebration of the feminine principle as solitary, somewhat magical in its access to knowledge, and exclusive of formal cultural affiliations—are very similar to those expressed by Eliot. Writing to Bodichon, she seems to identify her own position with Ruskin's, in implicit antagonism to the Davies position:

> I think Ruskin has not been encouraged about women by his many and persistent efforts to teach them. He seems to have found them wanting in real scientific interest—bent on sentimentalizing in everything.
>
> What I should like to be sure of as a result of higher education for women—a result that will come to pass over my grave—is, their recognition of the great amount of social unproductive labour which needs to be done by women, and which is now either not done at all or done wretchedly.
>
> No good can come to women, more than to any class of male mortals, while each aims at doing the highest kind of work, which ought rather to be held in sanctity as what only the few can do well. (VI:425)

As this letter suggests, Eliot identified not only with Ruskin's expression of a separate and glorified sphere for women but also with his anxiety that women are neglecting their "social unproductive labor."[6]

Eliot tends to become obscure in the presence of the Woman Question; here, the meaning of the phrase "social unproductive labor" is elusive. "Social labor" seems recognizable as the "queenly" duties of comforting and helping the poor and oppressed urged by Ruskin, yearned after by Dorothea Brooke, and practiced by Dinah Morris and Romola. But the word "unproductive" remains puzzling. This social labor must, in some sense, be "productive," inasmuch as it is envisioned as fulfilling a social need. The use of the negative term suggests the extent to which the positive term—"production"—has become associated with an "industrial view of life," that is, with the production specifically of commodities. If production and commodification are indeed so closely linked for Eliot that noncommodified labor cannot be referred to as "productive," then institutions for the production of knowledge are perilously close to being institutions for the commodification of knowledge.

The likeness of this view to Ruskin's, however, is qualified by Eliot's refusal to romanticize "social unproductive labor" and by the pessimism about its potential that her letter expresses. In describing social labor as "unproductive," Eliot refuses the comforts of the optimistic and hortatory meliorism of the program of "Of Queen's Gardens" and its implication that ambition can comfortably coexist with the demands of domestic ideology for female self-sacrifice. A similar refusal motivates her criticism of Geraldine Jewsbury's novel *Constance Herbert,* which she attacks for its suggestion that nothing renounced "'for the sake of a higher principle, will prove to have been worth the keeping.' . . . It is [the] very perception that the thing we renounce is precious, is something never to be compensated to us, which constitutes the beauty and heroism of renunciation" (*Selected Essays,* 321). In this review, written fifteen years before *Middlemarch,* "compensation" (like production, a word from the language of economic exchange) is already suspect.[7] Eliot's reference, in the letter to Bodichon, to her own grave, prefigures *Middlemarch's* closing image of "unvisited tombs": in Eliot's melancholy view, righteousness seems to guarantee, not recognition, but isolation. Renunciation for Eliot is less a recommended activity than a lost ideal that cannot exist in the realm of the productive or the compensatory; indeed, in *Middlemarch,* it is the longing for renunciation that is to be renounced by Dorothea, who, in a reversal of our usual understanding of renunciation, must give up the perilous career of the martyr for the comfortable role of parliamentary wife.

Eliot's analysis diverges in important ways from both Ruskin's and Davies's suggestions for female education. Although Eliot's ideals seems closer to Ruskin's than to Davies's, *Middlemarch* demonstrates the availability for commodification of both ideals. The commodification of Davies's ideal is perhaps more immediately apparent. Despite

Eliot's reticence about specific aspects of Davies's plans, it is difficult not to read *Middlemarch's* mockery of the Oxbridge tradition as partly a response to Davies's insistence that her new college for women should emulate the traditional Cambridge education. Casaubon is one of the products of that tradition, and the language of fog and claustrophobia associated with him refers not merely to his personal charmlessness; because his relationship to a particular system of classical learning and prosecution of knowledge is worked out and related in detail, that system is also the clear target of Eliot's satire. Together with Mr. Brooke and Fred Vincy, also men whom the unreformed Oxbridge system has rendered incompetent, Casaubon represents a fierce parody of the "dead hand" of traditional classical learning of the narrowest kind.

The education of Fred Vincy indicts an incurious reverence for higher education on the part of the bourgeoisie as well as the entrenched system of fellowships and religious exclusion that favored the production of impecunious curates whose main religious qualification might be a willingness to sign the Thirty-Nine Articles. The portrait of the Reverend Mr. Walter Stelling, M. A. Cantab., in *The Mill on the Floss,* and his education of Tom Tulliver makes a similar point in more detail. Despite his education, Stelling is conventionally mercenary, snobbish, and misogynist; worse yet, he is an unimaginative teacher, unable to tailor his lessons to the particular needs and capacities of his pupil, for whom Euclidean propositions and Latin grammar remain incomprehensibly abstract. It is Maggie, by her eager questions to Mr. Stelling when she visits, who forces into Tom's consciousness the "dim understanding of the fact that there had once been people upon the earth who were so fortunate as to know Latin without learning it through the medium of the Eton Grammar" (*Mill on the Floss,* 221). Tom has been denied this insight precisely because, as Eliot sarcastically observes, "Mr. Stelling was not the man to enfeeble and emasculate his pupil's mind by simplifying and explaining, or to reduce the tonic effect of etymology by mixing it with smattering, extraneous information such as is given to girls" (210). In other words, although Maggie views Tom's educational opportunities as a privilege from which she, by virtue of her gender, has been excluded, Eliot suggests that Maggie is unwittingly privileged in being excluded from an educational practice whose effect on Tom is entirely narrowing and stultifying.[8]

In *Middlemarch*, Fred Vincy is on his way to becoming a university product not unlike Stelling—"a curate in debt for horse-hire and cambric pocket-handkerchiefs," as Mary says (679). Like Tom, he discovers when he must make his living as Caleb Garth's assistant that the "gentleman's" education he has received has been worse than useless. "The deuce!" exclaims Garth, confronted with Fred's fashionably illegible handwriting, "to think that this is a country where a man's education may cost hundreds and hundreds, and it turns you out this!" (462). The two men in *Middlemarch* whose intellectual projects Eliot represents as truly serious, Ladislaw and Lydgate, have rejected traditional Oxbridge training: Ladislaw has chosen what his Uncle Casaubon calls "the anomalous course of studying at Heidelberg" (66) and subsequently wandering the Continent in search of culture; Lydgate's medical studies have taken him to London, Edinburgh, and Paris (119).

Eliot was by no means alone in the opinion that the classical education still favored by the universities would be a dubious prize for the new women scholars to win. Davies's insistence that her students maintain the traditional emphasis on classics and mathematics and prepare themselves for the existing examinations came close to alienating otherwise sympathetic reformers among Oxford and Cambridge dons. James Bryce, a professor of law at Oxford and a member of Hitchin's founding committee, wrote to Davies that he and others "think it a pity to load a new institution at starting with those very vices whose existence we deplore in an old one. In our view the course at your new College ought to be a model for men's Colleges to follow, instead of a slavish copy of their faults" (qtd. in Stephen, 156). Davies nevertheless resisted all separate-but-equal proposals, recognizing in them the lineaments of gratified domestic ideology. "Perhaps I exaggerate," she wrote to another supporter of different standards, "but I think it is discouraging to see so many of the new things for women started on the basis of separation. It seems like getting into more of a system of separateness, and it makes one suspicious of anything like a step in that direction" (qtd. in Stephen, 195). Davies's commitment to the Cambridge status quo and her essential indifference to its intellectual content underscores the distinction between her and Eliot in their conception of institutions. For Davies, the existence of the Oxbridge institution is the overwhelming fact; that institution is a means to self-determination. In *Middlemarch*, on the other hand, the institutionalized pursuit of knowledge by men is often coerced or wrongheaded and leads at best to comedy (Fred's confrontation with the Garths' expectations) and at worst to tragedy (Casaubon's misspent career), while self-determination, whether by women or by men, is revealed as largely a fiction.

If the portrayals of educated men in the novel cast doubt on the sufficiency of contemporary institutions of higher education, Eliot's portrait of Rosamond Vincy more directly anatomizes not only the dangers of the commodification of the Ruskinian domestic ideal but also that commodification's influence even over persons of putatively higher culture, such as Lydgate. Indeed, Rosamond, who reads "the best novels, and even the second best," memorizes not only Thomas Moore's *Lallah Rookh* but also the poetry of Scott, and spends her time "in being from morning till night her own standard of a perfect lady" (137), would, had she been born a little later, have made the perfect audience for Ruskin's criticism of middle-class complacency in "Of Queens' Gardens." But if Rosamond's imperviousness to the claims of others and the mercenary values of her education make her dangerous, it is the blindness of Lydgate, the scientific rationalist of modern education, that makes her fatal. Like Casaubon, in thinking about women, and particularly about marriage, Lydgate "get[s his] thoughts entangled in metaphors, and act[s] fatally on the strength of them" (70). This trait suggests that certain habits of thinking encouraged by domestic ideology—particularly, judging live women by the standard of the metaphorical Woman—can be dangerous. This caution about allowing metaphors to become reified as unconsidered ideology is at odds, if not with the values of "Of Queens' Gardens," then certainly with the aesthetic form in which they are presented.

The aspect of Ruskin's aesthetic with which Eliot most identified was his "realism—the doctrine that all truth and beauty are to be attained by a humble and faithful study of nature, and not by substituting vague forms, bred by imagination on the mists of feeling, in place of definite, substantial reality." She goes on, in her review of his *Modern Painters,* volume 3, to add the qualification that truth must "be so taught as to compel men's attention and sympathy. . . . Mr. Ruskin has a voice . . . of such power, that whatever error he may mix with his truth, he will make more converts to that truth than less erring advocates who are hoarse and feeble. . . . The vigor and splendour of his eloquence are not more remarkable than its precision, and the delicate truthfulness of his epithets" (*Selected Essays,* 368–69).

"Eloquence" refers in its root sense to spoken, rather than written, expression; and it is not surprising that stylistics of "eloquence" are marked in "Of Queen's Gardens," originally a lecture with a hortatory purpose—to inspire philanthropy. For example, Ruskin builds the final section around an extended flower metaphor, a development marked by his assertion of its literality:

> The path of a good woman is indeed strewn with flowers; but they rise behind her steps, not before them. "Her feet have touched the meadows, and left the daisies rosy."
>
> You think that only a lover's fancy; false and vain! How if it could be true? You think this also, perhaps, only a poet's fancy—"even the light harebell raised its head / Elastic from her airy tread." But it is little to say of a woman, that she only does not destroy where she passes. She should revive; the harebells should bloom, not stoop, as she passes. You think I am rushing into hyperbole? Pardon me, not a whit; I mean what I say in calm English, spoken in resolute truth. (176)

Ruskin continues to elaborate the metaphor, conjuring "flowers that could bless you for having blessed them, and will love you for having loved them; flowers that have thoughts like yours and lives like yours, and which, once saved, you save forever" (177). This flower imagery constitutes a conventional practice (the comparison of women with flowers) that Ruskin might have expected his listeners to find familiar and flattering. Furthermore, the fanciful floral language might disguise the fact that he was asking his middle-class audience to confront the less attractive reality of prostitution—just as, according to Rosamond Vincy, flower petals were strewn in wealthy homes to disguise a sickroom smell. But Eliot's portrait of Rosamond Vincy reveals a weakness in the rhetoric of Ruskin's appeal. The difficulty is not Eliot believes metaphor to be *per se* opposed to realism.[9] Rather, what Eliot demonstrates in *Middlemarch* is that metaphors about women, like the values of domestic ideology, are all too easily subject to an unreflecting hypostatization by middle-class subjects who will fall back on them as a substitute for understanding or analysis of individual or class responsibilities.

Eliot's use of the flower metaphor in *Middlemarch* is apparently more conventional than Ruskin's. Her flowers are not downtrodden working-class women to be ministered to, but middle-class women themselves. On our first meeting with Rosamond—the worldly rose, as her name reminds us—we are told that she is "admitted to be the flower of Mrs. Lemon's school" (78), and flower imagery subsequently multiplies around her, particularly in her relationship to Lydgate. She appears to Lydgate at their first meeting "as if the petals of some gigantic flower had just opened and disclosed her" (13); when she cries on the occasion that leads to their engagement, her tears are "like water on a blue flower"; "looking at those Forget-me-nots under the water," Lydgate is lost (247). During the engagement, Eliot describes her as being "in the water-lily's expanding wonderment at its own fuller life" (284). Discussing the shortening of that engagement, she "blushed and looked at [Lydgate] as the garden flowers look at us when we walk forth happily among them in the transcendent evening light: is there not a soul," Eliot interrupts to ask, apparently rhetorically, "beyond utterance, half-nymph, half-child, in those delicate petals which glow and breathe about the centres of deep colour?" (289). But this question turns out not be rhetorical: the answer is "No." Elaborating that answer after the marriage of Rosamond and Lydgate, Eliot begins fully to reveal the intransigence of the soul hidden below Rosamond's petal-like surface. A closing image of Rosamond as simultaneously flower and bird removes her utterly and sinisterly from the realm of the human: "As the years went by [Lydgate] opposed her less and less, whence Rosamond concluded that he had learned the value of her opinion. . . instead of the threatened cage in Bride Street [he had] provided one all flowers and gilding, fit for the bird of paradise that she resembled." The botanical image turns murderous as the passage continues: "He once called her his basil plant; and when she asked for an explanation, said that basil was a plant which had flourished wonderfully on a murdered man's brains" (680). Lydgate becomes a fashionable doctor and dies of diphtheria at fifty; the flowerlike Rosamond turns out to be, not an ornament, but a toxin to the man whose fate is attached to hers.

It is true, of course, that Eliot lays some of the blame for Rosamond and Lydgate's misalliance at the door of Lydgate himself. Although he is educated, cosmopolitan, and unconventional in his intellectual pursuits, he is "common" in his beliefs about women: "He was no radical in relation to anything but medical reform and the prosecution of discovery. In the rest of practical life he walked by hereditary habit; half from that personal pride and unreflecting egoism which I have already called commonness, and half from that naiveté which belongs to preoccupation with favorite ideas" (286). This glance at "hereditary habit" and the revelation of the flower imagery attaching to Rosamond as essentially empty are the nearest Eliot comes to arraigning patriarchal attitudes. Lydgate's thoughts about Rosamond, like her education itself, are a satire of the model of "accomplishment" that represented the least morally serious, and most continuously deprecated, version of women's education from the mid-eighteenth century on: "An accomplished woman," Lydgate tells Rosamond, "almost always knows more than we men, though her knowledge is of a different sort. I am sure you could teach me a thousand things—as an exquisite bird could teach a bear if there were any common language between them. Happily, there is a common language between women and men, and so the bears can get taught" (131). His zoological distinction later comes back to haunt him, when he is forced to reflect that "she no more identified herself with him than if they had been creatures of different species and opposing interests" (487). The birds and the bears, cannot, after all, communicate.

Lydgate's reliance upon "hereditary habit" in thinking about women represents a form of mental laziness. He reserves his idealism for his work, with the result that his expectations of marriage to Rosamond partake of no higher an ideal than hers. In Rosamond, he congratulates himself upon the possession of "a half-opened blush rose . . . adorned with accomplishments for the refined amusement of man" (221). Lydgate's expectations of womanhood, the narrator implies, ensure and partly deserve their own frustration. More serious, perhaps, than the ruin of Lydgate's ambitions is the demonstration that even his scientific rationalism, which the novel certainly admires, is susceptible to the garden-variety fantasies of the cultural imagination. In his intellectual life, Lydgate is moved by genuine scientific passion to devise the most up-to-date course of study possible; yet he is fatally deficient in the education of the heart, a deficiency that can only be remedied by an experience which, like the heroic medical practice he deprecates, may have the unfortunate side effect of total destruction.

Although Eliot attaches a degree of blame to Lydgate for his mistaken marriage, he nevertheless is represented as a victim of Rosamond's allure, "that combination of correct sentiments, music, dancing, drawing, elegant note-writing, private album for extracted verse, and perfect blonde loveliness, which made the irresistible woman for the doomed man of that date" (221). Because Lydgate has intellectual aspirations, which the reader does evaluate as "higher" than his marital ones and than Rosamond's, and because he shares with the reader the experience of being educated by the events of the novel, the reader identifies with him and feels allied with him against Rosamond. To the extent that he is the target of Eliot's dramatic irony, his "spots of commonness" seem more an appropriately domestic form of hubris than an indictment of his character. Even when Lydgate or the narrator expresses pity for Rosamond, that pity is likely to have the same effect on the reader that it does on Lydgate himself: "He wished to excuse everything in her if he could—but it was inevitable that in that excusing mood he should think of her as if she were an animal of another and feebler species" (546). Rosamond—the mermaid, the waternixie, the "feebler species"—becomes a creature with whom the reader can hardly identify.

It might be argued that Eliot's portrait of Rosamond in itself represents an argument for the better education of women. As I suggested in chapter 1, a common reformist argument strategically derived the urgency of educating middle-class women at least partly from the pernicious effects on middle-class domesticity of the incongruence between male and female intellectual training. Emily Davies, for example, observes that "[s]ocial and domestic intercourse is an educational instrument largely used in cultivated circles. In the great mass of English society it is scarcely used at all, for this obvious reason, that education is in great part onesided, and the easy interchange of thought is therefore impossible" (*Higher Education*, 114–15). Such observations suggest that the reform of women's education will enhance, rather than threaten, the values of domestic ideology. Addressing the same topic in *The Subjection of Women,* John Stuart Mill goes beyond presenting the gap between male and female intellect as a mere social discomfort to the suggestion that women's degraded intelligence has a contaminating force: "Men of the greatest promise generally cease to improve as soon as they marry, and, not improving, inevitably degenerate. If the wife does not push the husband forward, she always holds him back" (235).[10]

Feminist reformers clearly used the fear of women's contaminating shallowness of intellect to urge their integration into corporate intellectual life. This argument was not foolproof, however; it was perfectly possible to grant the premise that women were deficiently educated without granting that they should therefore be educated in institutions similar to men's. Many writers stressed the necessity for isolating, rather than training, the inferior female intellect. Writers as different as Mary Wollstonecraft and Sarah Stickney Ellis, for example, both deplore the influence of boarding school life on girls. Charlotte Yonge refused to lend her name to the support of Girton because she had "decided objections to bringing large masses of girls together" (Caine, 87). Eliot seems to reject both solutions—incorporation and isolation—in favor of a rather magically conceived heterosexual intellectual union. The most successful marriages in *Middlemarch* feature an equality of intellectual interests and expectations between husband and wife (Will and Dorothea; Fred and Mary; even Sir James and Celia). That equality, however, owes nothing to equal participation in educational institutions or an equality of intellectual opportunities; rather, it appears to be temperamental.

Finally, the narrative animus toward Rosamond exceeds our ability to view her as a victim of social forces. The excess motivation of that animus is surely the class anxiety that informed the Victorian debates over higher education in general. *Middlemarch*'s reviewer R. H. Hutton objected that Rosamond represented "a type of wom[a]n far too unique to be much of a contribution towards the woman question" (qtd. in Carroll, 308). In fact, however, the portrait of Rosamond's education and its effects is the novel's most conventional satire. Mrs. Lemon is a direct descendant of Thackeray's Miss Pinkerton of Chiswick Mall. Although such satire is based on salient criticisms of girls' education still germane by 1870,[11] it also reflects a cultural uneasiness with the spectacle of the socially, professionally, or intellectually ambitious woman. Society had both institutional mechanisms (e.g., universities, political parties) and beliefs (the Evangelical emphasis on labor) that evolved to adapt to and even celebrate the figure of the self-made man. But the figure of the self-made woman, or the woman attempting to make herself, was more troubling. A woman who wanted to raise her class status could do so only by marrying, but an overt admission that marriage might be undertaken for such a reason undermined the romantic and compensatory principle according to which the domestic angel was not the ambitious man's cocompetitor, but his reward.[12]

The Vincy parents are cheerfully explicit about the meaning of their pecuniary investment in both Fred's and Rosamond's educations. Rosamond's father, unimpressed by Lydgate's gentility unsupported by wealth, asks: "What have you had such an education for, if you are to go and marry a poor man? It's a cruel thing for a father to see" (290). In Eliot's representation, the elder Vincys' honest pursuit of material comfort reads as preferable to the muddled self-delusion of Rosamond's social aspiration: "The piquant fact about Lydgate was his good birth, which . . . presented marriage as a prospect of rising in rank and getting a little nearer to that celestial condition on earth in which she would have nothing to do with vulgar people, and perhaps at last associate with relatives quite equal to the county people who looked down on the Middlemarchers" (136). Neither set of aspirations is admirable, but the parents' is more open, and therefore less pernicious, in its understanding of both education and marriage as means to a material end. The veneer of romance and gentility that covers Rosamond's social ambitions —disguising them, to some degree, even from herself—makes them far more dangerous, as Lydgate discovers.

The Vincy parents—though not their children—belong to the immediate, eighteenth-century past, represented in this novel by Henry Fielding, for which Eliot feels such nostalgia. Throughout *Middlemarch,* Eliot's sympathies are not so much at one or the other end of the industrial middle-class spectrum, which is all contaminated by commodification, as with an alternative and vanishing agrarian model of social relationships within which the Brookes and the Garths—both families peripheral to Middlemarch proper—both dwell. Contrasting the portrayal of Rosamond Vincy with that of Celia Brooke reveals the degree to which Eliot's distaste for Rosamond as the product of a finishing-school education emerges specifically from an anxiety about modern *embourgeoisement*. The intellectual content of Celia's education at Lausanne "on plans at once narrow and promiscuous" (8) is no more impressive than that of Rosamond's which emulates it: its most observable result is the ability to play "an 'air, with variations,' a small kind of tinkling which symbolized the aesthetic part of the young ladies' education" (37). But Rosamond's far greater musical talent is depicted as dangerous, part of her actress's ability to assume virtues of sensibility that she doesn't have, while Celia's innocent worldliness and entrenched vapidity have none of the destructive effects of Rosamond's similar qualities.

This distinction makes Rosamond far more important to the narrative than Celia. The essential difference between the two girls' educations seems to be that Celia's is designed to consolidate, and Rosamond's to penetrate, social boundaries; in marrying Sir James, Celia achieves not an elevation but an alliance of class. But Celia's graceful assumption of the role of Lady Chettham has the narrative disadvantage of complete irrelevance to *Middlemarch*'s schema of conflict, and Eliot treats her with increasing impatience thereafter. Eliot is more concerned with the failures than with the successes of education in producing subjects who can reconcile the competing moral imperatives of self-actualization and social commitment. Rosamond and Dorothea both represent more explosive relations to those competing moral imperatives.

In that sense, the novel's fair femme fatale and its dark heroine, perhaps surprisingly, begin their narratives in positions more parallel than opposed. Both the worldly and vacuous Rosamond and the spiritual and "intellectually consequent" Dorothea have, as the novel begins, recently concluded their formal educations—a procedure that has entirely failed to check the delusion of each about the peculiar centrality of her own subjectivity. At the same time, both women are at the mercy of equally delusory expectations of the significance of their gender held even by persons of quite extensive education, such as Casaubon and Lydgate. In other words, Rosamond and Dorothea both overestimate the power of their will toward self-definition (as particular persons); the persons surrounding them overestimate the power of the social will to interpellate them as exemplary subjects (Women); and the education whose ideal function, as Eliot imagines it, would be to mediate these claims and constitute the resulting compromise as morality has failed in that role. Over the course of the novel, Dorothea learns her lesson, through learning that the object of knowledge is not, as she had originally believed, Latin and Greek, not even the more socially useful housing design schemes for which she has a genuine talent, but the limitations of the self. Rosamond, of course, learns neither this nor any other lesson: "She simply continued to be mild in her temper, inflexible in her judgment, disposed to admonish her husband, and able to frustrate him by stratagem. As the years went on he opposed her less and less, whence Rosamond concluded that he had learned the value of her opinion" (679). This inability to change in her own opinions, in a novel that valorizes such change even when the price is paid in careers and ambitions, is another characteristic that renders Rosamond unsympathetic.

Like Rosamond, Dorothea feels undervalued in her immediate social circle; like Rosamond, she imagines that marriage will reward her true worth: "She was looking forward to higher initiation into ideas, as she was looking forward to marriage, and blending her dim conceptions of both" (70). Accepting Casaubon's marriage proposal, she exclaims, "'I am very ignorant—you will quite wonder at my ignorance . . . I have so many thoughts that may be quite mistaken; and now I shall be able to tell them all to you, and ask you about them'" (41). The irony, of course, is that her ignorance lies in a different direction than she imagines. As Celia observes, "since this engagement . . . cleverness seemed . . . more pitiable than ever" (67). Dorothea's attempts to remedy her premarital ignorance by learning Latin and Greek are not less misguided than Rosamond's single-minded focus on her trousseau; furthermore, Eliot is ruefully skeptical even of Dorothea's altruism: "It was not entirely out of devotion to her future husband that she wished to know Latin and Greek. . . . [S]he had not reached that point of renunciation at which she would have been satisfied with having a wise husband: she wished, poor child, to be wise herself" (52).

Although Eliot acknowledges Dorothea's naive self-deception, she is not willing to let us think her protagonist might be intellectually ambitious. Just a few chapters later, she assures us: "It would be a great mistake to suppose that Dorothea would have cared about any share in Mr. Casaubon's learning as mere accomplishment. . . . All her eagerness for acquirement lay within that full current of sympathetic motive in which her ideas and impulses were habitually swept along" (70). The desire for knowledge as an ethical grounding that lies beneath Dorothea's apparently selfless and appropriately feminine devotion to her husband is equally selfless, if not equally passive. Eliot does not suggest that either impulse is misguided; nevertheless, both represent the "moral stupidity" out of which Dorothea must be schooled. Yet on the novel's own terms, the moral necessity for the renunciation of all of Dorothea's aims, such as the village which would be a "school of industry," which Brooke and Chettham dissuade her from founding (626), is not obvious. No ethical reason emerges for Dorothea's final failure to return with greater clarity to what was genuinely morally noble in her aims, which she buries in her marriage to Will.

It would be wrong to conclude, however, that Eliot simply subsumes intellectual to ethical development, or active philanthropy to passive magnanimity. The connections among these impulses are maintained in a set of images that persists in Dorothea's narrative, images that associate both romantic and intellectual fulfillment with the physical space of the library, the most important and frequently mentioned interior in Dorothea's narrative. At the beginning of the novel, oppressed by Celia's worldly perspicacities, Dorothea finds comfort there in the religious monographs her uncle brings her: "I have brought a couple of pamphlets for you, Dorothea—in the library, you know; they lie on the table in the library." At these words, "[t]he oppression of Celia, Tantripp, and Sir James was shaken off and she walked straight to the library. . . . When [Mr. Brooke] reentered the library, he found Dorothea seated and already deep in one of the pamphlets which had some marginal manuscript of Mr. Casaubon's—taking it in as eagerly as she might have taken in the scent of a fresh bouquet after a dry, hot, dreary walk." The scene, with its emphasis on the distinction between Dorothea and less serious women who find bouquets more refreshing than "pamphlets about the Early Church" (31), begins an identification of the library with Dorothea's intellectual and emotional development that persists throughout the novel. It is in her uncle's library, for example, that Dorothea receives Casaubon's epistolary proposal, and to the library that she returns to deliver her note of acceptance.

If the library at Tipton Grange—warmed by Brooke's fire and the bumbling good nature that reminds him to bring religious pamphlets home to Dorothea—is a brief retreat from the "petty courses" of Middlemarch and its environs and apparently the anteroom to a life of "larger duties," the library at Lowick soon shows itself to be the most suffocating of chambers. There Dorothea and Casaubon argue over Ladislaw's letter; there Casaubon first collapses. Dorothea's memorable encounters with Lydgate (that in which he tells her of her husband's condition, and that in which he tells her of his own resolve to abandon the hospital and leave Middlemarch), both of which have as their theme the defeat of intellectual ambition, also take place there: "When Lydgate begged to speak with her alone, Dorothea opened the library door which happened to be nearest. . . . It was the first time she had entered this room since her husband had been taken ill, and the servant had chosen not to open the shutters. But there was light enough to read by from the narrow upper panes of the windows" (236–37). This darkness, of course, is symptomatic: During Casaubon's illness, Dorothea shuts herself up in the library transcribing his notes. "I wish every book in that library was built into a caticomb [*sic*] for your master," says Dorothea's maid to Casaubon's valet (393)—percipiently, since Casaubon rather fancies such a "caticomb" in his memory: "He willingly imagined [Dorothea] toiling under the fetters of a promise to erect a tomb with his name upon it" (403).

It is, therefore, to the library that Dorothea returns to free herself after his death, rejecting the promise that Casaubon attempted to extract from her before his death, and writing him a note that reads, in part, "*Do you not see now that I could not submit my soul to yours, by working hopelessly at what I have no belief in?*" (440). In learning to have "no belief in" Casaubon's project, Dorothea has learned the limitations of her own naive definition of "wisdom." With this act begins the redemption of the library as a place of intellectual and emotional freedom, as its association with Casaubon's "mouldy futilities" (168) gives way to an association with Will Ladislaw's more dilettante, but more passionate and cosmopolitan, conception of knowledge. Dorothea's confrontation with Ladislaw in this library after Casaubon's codicil has destroyed their friendship begins the trajectory that will finally unite them. The second meeting with Lydgate impels the visits to Rosamond that end by clearing Will of the implications of flirtation. Most important, however, is the gothic scene of reconciliation between Will and Dorothea. When Will comes to bid her a last farewell, "it crossed her mind that she could not receive him in this library, where her husband's prohibition seemed to dwell" (658). But a storm prevents her from meeting him outside and turns the room into a literally electric scene of recognition: "While he was speaking there came a vivid flash of lightning which lit each of them up for the other—and the light seemed to be the terror of a hopeless love. Dorothea darted instantaneously from the window; Will followed her, seizing her hand with a spasmodic movement; and so they stood, with their hands clasped, like two children, looking out on the storm" (661). This Brontë-esque display of natural disturbance breaks open the "stone prison" of Lowick and reestablishes the library as a genuine scene of fulfillment and the reconciliation of intellectual and emotional needs.

In making the library, rather than the drawing room or the boudoir (the two rooms in which Rosamond is always to be found), the most significant physical space for Dorothea, Eliot asserts the primacy of her intellectual life. She also evokes Ruskin's vision of the isolated girl wandering in the library, "tak[ing] her own fair form and way if she take any." Dorothea, like the heroine of Ruskin's imagination, remains aloof from corporate educational projects, or identification with other women; but, also like Ruskin's heroine, she nevertheless manages to conjure romantic as well as intellectual sustenance in this intensely private space. In literalizing, in the weather, the notion that Ladislaw is "storming" the library, Eliot perhaps hints at the difficulties of sexual and intellectual isolation as a preparation for the project of romantic union.

It is notoriously difficult for the reader to experience the union of Dorothea and Will as a fulfillment and reconciliation, especially given the free-floating melancholy that characterizes the novel's subsequent conclusion. Contemporary feminist critics have objected to the diminishment of Dorothea's ambitions, but, as Gillian Beer points out, the problem is not a only modern one. She cites Sidney Colvin's criticism from 1873: "There is no sense of triumph in [Dorothea's marriage to Ladislaw]; there is rather a sense of sadness in a subdued and restricted, if not now a thwarted destiny" (qtd. in Beer, 152). That difficulty does not lessen when the narrative is looked at from the point of view of the educational project. Although Will early opens Dorothea's eyes to the aridity of Casaubon's exegetical method, he himself is associated less with any alternative system of education or knowledge than with the dilettante cosmopolitanism with which Dorothea never shows any particular sympathy.[13] Although Eliot clearly admires Will, the novel does not embed him in a complex intellectual structure, the way it does Lydgate. Dorothea's own unaided intellectual efforts, meanwhile, are not much less comic than Celia's. Her theological and architectural researches simply evaporate after her first marriage. In our last view of her alone in the library, before Will enters, we find her studying geography:

A map was a fine thing to study when you were disposed to think of something else, being made up of names that would turn into a chime if you went back upon them. Dorothea set earnestly to work, bending close to her map, and uttering the names in an audible, subdued tone, which often got into a chime. She looked amusingly girlish after all her deep experience—nodding her head and marking the names off on her fingers, with a little pursing of her lip, and now and them breaking off to put her hands on each side of her face and say, "Oh dear! oh dear!" (658)

This scene makes trivial Dorothea's earlier intellectual ambitions—a kind of diminution that, before her marriage, she angrily resisted: "Poor Dodo," says Celia, "it is your favourite fad to draw plans." Dorothea responds: "Fad to draw plans! Do you think I only care about my fellow creatures' houses in that childish way?" (31). In this later scene, however, Eliot represents her studies as precisely this sort of childish pastime.

If neither Will nor Dorothea seems to define an entirely satisfying or specifiable intellectual model, then it is not surprising that their union also fails to do so. Beer has suggested that in moving from Casaubon to Will, Dorothea "abandon[s] the role of mentor and pupil as a kind of father and daughter" for a relationship in which the lovers "educate each other." Certainly it is true that "[t]he book itself resists the usual punitive outcome for lovers who educate each other which is shown in the stories of Francesca and Paulo, Abelard and Heloise, Julie and St Preux." However, when Beer goes on to argue that "lovers cannot be relied on as educators. Institutions are essential" (174), she seems to be imputing a belief shared by reformers contemporary with Eliot to Eliot herself, somewhat in the teeth of the evidence of a novel that, as I have suggested, depicts not a single successful educational institution. The main educational model of *Middlemarch,* largely moral rather than intellectual, is the relational one to which Beer first points: Mary Garth and Farebrother educate Fred Vincy by way of his "love problem"; Dorothea and Lydgate are educated, however painfully, by their entanglements with Casaubon and Rosamond; Susan and Mary Garth are utopian mothers who provide models of maternal pedagogy that tend to deprecate, if not preempt, formal education: "Mary . . . gave the boys little formal teaching. . . . Nevertheless, they were found quite forward enough when they went to school; perhaps, because they had liked nothing so well as being with their mother" (679). What is striking about such an affective model of education is that it is completely resistant, by definition, to institutionalization.

Indeed, lack of interruption from precisely such affective relations was one of the qualities of life at Girton stressed by Emily Davies. In a prospectus entitled "Some Account of a Proposed College for Women" (1868), she wrote:

> Each student will have a small sitting-room to herself, where she will be free to study undisturbed, and to enjoy at her discretion the companionship of friends of her own choice. Of all the attractions offered by the college life, probably the opportunity for a certain amount of solitude, so necessary an agent in the formation of character, will be the one most welcomed by the real student. . . . [M]ost of the members of the college will come there very much for the sake of temporary seclusion. (Qtd. in Stephen, 176)

Stephen suggests that Davies's "longing for privacy was in reality a longing for freedom" (176). Such privacy was, paradoxically, the antidote to the isolation many intellectually ambitious women felt in the enforced company of their families and social peers who did not share their interests. "Miss Lumsden said that before she came [to Girton]," Davies wrote, "she used to feel fearfully solitary. She was always having said to her, 'Oh, but you're so exceptional.' Now, she feels herself belonging to a body, and has lost the sense of loneliness" (qtd. in Stephen, 235).

In Eliot's work, too, despite the emergence of a relational model of moral education, a similar longing for privacy and freedom may be discerned.[14] For her, however, the institutional model is no solution; she both idealizes the family ties that to Davies are a burden and seems unable to imagine corporate forms of existence—Dorothea's model village never gets off the ground, and ministering reformers such as Romola and Dinah rarely act communally. At the same time, they do not remain alone: Romola becomes the mother to both her husband's lover and their illegitimate child; Dinah marries Adam and gives up preaching. Eliot can valorize the self-taught, intellectually ambitious woman, as long as she does not challenge the primacy of family ties.

In *Middlemarch,* the character who most successfully inhabits this position is not Dorothea, but Mary Garth. Mary, like Eliot herself, is an intellectual woman—a reader, and finally an author, of fiction; also like Eliot, she remains mistrustful and impatient of intellectual institutions. Novel reading is as closely associated with privacy and self-development for both Mary and Eliot as having one's personal study is for Davies. Where for Davies, the corporate power of the institution seems necessary to protect self-development against encroaching familial demands, for Eliot, corporate bonds are as onerous as familial ones, and less morally compelling. "I have tried being a teacher," Mary observes, "and I am not fit for that: my mind is too fond of wandering on its own way" (112).[15] Mary finds all the solitude she needs in the act of reading, as her domineering employer Peter Featherstone irritably intuits: "She was for reading when she sat with me. But I put a stop to that. She's got the newspaper to read out loud. That's enough for one day, I should think. I can't abide to see her reading to herself" (91). Featherstone "can't abide" Mary's reading because he sees that Mary-the-reader, unlike Mary-the-companion, is beyond his control—beyond his control without physical removal or specifiable resistance. Indeed, reading in *Middlemarch* is the minimal material extrusion of a struggle for self-definition whose impulse is generally almost entirely internal.[16] It is the most portable and private resistance to one's current surroundings or escape into different ones. And yet—equally minimally—it puts the alienated reader in contact with others who share her sensibility; others who, unlike the residents of a college, have the advantage of not really existing and therefore present no possible encroachment on the self.

Mary Garth's reading is determined neither by the elite possession of a private library, such as Dorothea enjoys (how many of Ruskin's listeners, one wonders, comfortable though they were, had an "old library" in which to turn their daughters loose?), nor by participation in Middlemarch's circulating library, to which we are emphatically assured that she does not belong (257). Mentioned in the context of the money-hungry relations who huddle at Stone Court awaiting Featherstone's death, the circulating library is clearly associated with the commodification not only of literature but also of the moral sympathy that literature is supposed to inspire. Mary is nevertheless surrounded by books, particularly novels, throughout *Middlemarch;* and one of her functions is to help the reader learn to distinguish between the appropriate and inappropriate uses of literary experience, and particularly the experience of the novel. Educational reformers had mixed feelings about novel reading. For Davies, "heterogeneous reading" is one of the dilettante occupations that impedes women's serious intellectual study (*Higher Education,* 58). For Ruskin, who did not believe serious intellectual study to be necessary for women, girls' reading could be self-regulating, so long as the distinction between "good" and "light" literature were observed:

> Only let us be sure that her books are not heaped up in her
> lap as they fall out of the package of the circulating library,
> wet with the last and lightest spray of the fountain of folly. . . .
>
> I speak, therefore, of good novels only, and our modern liter-
> ature is particularly rich in types of such. Well read, indeed,
> these books have serious use, being nothing less than treatises
> on moral anatomy and chemistry; studies of human nature in
> the elements of it. ("Of Queens' Gardens," 156, 157)

As Ruskin's distinction suggests, in the absence of participation in those public institutions that shape an individual's relationship to culture, novel reading—properly regulated—could be a kind of substitute contact with the wider world. To Eliot's heroines, the solitary, relished reading of novels offers an emotional and intellectual vocabulary, especially those, like Mary Garth and Maggie Tulliver, whose provincial circumstances most closely resemble Eliot's own.

The habit of "moral anatomy" serves Mary Garth, for example, well. Importuned by Fred Vincy to contradict the proposition that "a woman is never in love with any one she has always known," she parries:

> "Let me see . . . I must go back on my experience. There
> is Juliet—she seems an example of what you say. But then
> Ophelia had probably known Hamlet a long while; and
> Brenda Troil—she had known Mordaunt Merton ever since
> they were children; but then he seems to have been an

estimable young man; and Minna was still more deeply in love with Cleveland, who was a stranger. Waverley was new to Flora MacIvor, but then she did not fall in love with him. And there are Olivia and Sophia Primrose, and Corinne—they may be said to have fallen in love with new men. Altogether, my experience is rather mixed." (114)

Mary is being arch, as Eliot says; but she is also using literature to hold her own in the face of Fred's premature lovemaking: she has learned a great deal from the generally tragic careers of those heroines. Her reading lists seem rather like attempts to define a newly emerging field of English literature—Scott, Shakespeare, and Goldsmith (and one French woman, de Staël). Indeed, Scott and Shakespeare seem to represent a golden mean between the pedagogical failings of Dorothea's religious pamphlets, on the one hand, as exemplified in Dorothea's unrealizable yearnings after martyrdom, and "light" literature on the other, as exemplified by Rosamond's equally naive conception of "romance," in which "it was not necessary to imagine much about the inward life of a hero, or of his serious business in the world" (136). These authors, like Eliot herself, encourage Ruskin's "studies of human nature in the elements of it."

We might expect that the valorization of the novel over the educational institution, and the autodidact over the university student, would also authorize the self-projection of the novelist as aesthetic and moral instructor. But if reading in Eliot is an almost surprisingly positive act, precisely because of its private nature, writing—the much more overt claim of the intellectual woman on public space—is more ambivalently represented. Anxiety about authorship is all over Middlemarch. "If [Dorothea] had written a book," Eliot early—and without provocation—assures us, "she must have done it as Saint Theresa did, under the command of an authority that constrained her conscience" (70–71). The assurance is odd because writing a book is not one of the activities toward which Dorothea is tempted, though it might well have been more achievable than founding a Fourierist village. It is Mary Garth who publishes "a little book [originally written for] her boys, called Stories of Great Men, Taken From Plutarch" (677); the work is locally attributed to Fred, as his agricultural study is attributed to Mary. This joke on Middlemarch's evaluative capabilities more seriously serves to relieve Mary from the charge of possible egoism lurking within authorship; further, Mary's is a "little" book, conceived for a domestic purpose and establishing a vernacular relationship to classical learning very different from Dorothea's early yearnings after dead languages.

In the final analysis, the model of the autodidact as embodied in Mary Garth is both idiosyncratic and mythologized. Mary's moral wisdom, unlike Dorothea's, is fixed before we ever meet her, and it is apparently attributable to her upbringing in an obsolete, and nostalgically rendered, domestic pastoral. Mary begins as a modern figure straight from the pages of the *English Woman's Journal:* the clever girl who must earn her bread and dreads the usual option open to her. "'Mary Garth can bear being [Featherstone's companion] at Stone Court, because she likes that better than being a governess,'" Rosamond points out to her mother (83). But she is the product of an organic rural household of an old-fashioned type. Her mother—herself a former governess—easily unites thorough housewifery with home schooling:

> Mrs. Garth at certain hours was always in the kitchen, and this morning she was carrying on several occupations at once there—making her pies at the well-scoured deal table on one side of that airy room, observing Sally's movements at the oven and dough-tub through the open door, and giving lessons to her youngest boy and girl, who were standing opposite to her at the table with their books and slates before them. (201)

This is the sort of scene whose obsolescence among middle-class families Emily Davies, by 1866, is politely pointing out: "The married ladies of former days, instead of sitting in drawing-rooms, eating the bread of idleness, got through a vast amount of household business, which their successors cannot possibly do, simply because it is not there to be done" (*Higher Education,* 103); and, she might have added, because it has become déclassé for them to do it. Mary Garth, after her marriage to Fred, supplements a perhaps diminished amount of "household business" with her writing. But in any case, by the end of the novel, she has become a mythic figure:

On inquiry it might possibly be found that Fred and Mary still inhabit Stone Court—that the creeping plants still cast the foam of their blossoms over the fine stone-wall into the field where the walnut-trees stand in stately row—and that on sunny days the lovers who were first engaged with the umbrella-ring may be seen in white-haired placidity at the open window from which Mary Garth, in the days of old Peter Featherstone, had often been ordered to look out for Mr. Lydgate. (679)

Through the power of this timeless pastoral even "old Peter Feather-stone" himself, a money-grubbing tyrant in life, takes on a venerable aura, and Fred and Mary leave behind entirely the novel's general mode of psychological realism.

However, the plenitude of this nostalgic image barely conceals a more melancholy mood; for nostalgia in Middlemarch recedes end-lessly.[17] It might seem at first reading that the nostalgia experienced by the reader of the 1870s is simply for the agrarian, prereform 1830s of the setting, with the concluding image of Stone Court a freeze-frame of that time. But *Middlemarch* is suffused with a longing for a past even be-fore the time of its setting, and it is that past to which Stone Court seems to be referred: some truly pastoral past which is the subject of Eliot's encomium to Fielding, who "lived when the days were longer (for time, like money, is measured by our needs), when summer after-noons were spacious, and the clock ticked slowly in the winter evenings" (116). And the novel's nostalgia goes even beyond Fielding to the time of St. Theresa; beyond that, to the time of Antigone. Such longings are unironized when voiced by the narrator, but Dorothea's own yearning for previous eras of greatness is mocked, and her longing to "lead a grand life—here—now—in England" (24) on the model of those heroic eras is revealed as self-delusion. The irony is compounded if we re-member that both St. Theresa and Antigone expressed nostalgia for past orders in which loyalty to faith or family transcended pragmatic or political concerns. This infinitely regressive nostalgia works against the development of solutions to the problems raised by the narrative. Nei-ther the organic, pastoral social relations represented by "Fielding" and "the Garths," nor the opportunities for moral solitude offered by the so-cially streamlined landscapes of feudal England and the Greek state seem to offer a useful model for subjects living within the complex social relations of nineteenth-century England.[18]

If we set side by side Davies's determination to scale, on women's behalf, the high walls of masculine privilege surrounding Oxbridge, and Eliot's skepticism about institutions and idealization of women's social unproductive labor, it is possible to see them as diametrically opposed: Eliot conservative and nostalgic, Davies liberal and forward-looking. This contrast, however, is easy to counter: Davies was a lifelong Conservative, Eliot profoundly concerned with contemporary epistemologies. Rather, the differences between the two women lie in their conceptions of the individual, which bring each one closer to one of the two competing Victorian conceptions of subjectivity: liberal individualism and domestic ideology.

For Davies, individuals, including individual women, became intelligible and consequent largely through the medium of public activity, which she understood positively as a process of adjustment and cooperation that did not necessitate rebellion or a thorough rejection of convention. This understanding of the subject is certainly close to the liberal individualist model, although with a distinct deemphasis of that model's oppositional character. Eliot, on the other hand, was thoroughly imbued with the opposition between individual and social needs inherent in the individualist view of the subject. Frequently reiterating the sentiment that "there is no creature whose inward being is so strong that it is not greatly determined by what lies outside it" (682), she assumes that this relationship must be one of conflict rather than cooperation. Renunciation or rebellion are the only options for Eliot's "inward being," under constant pressure from an essentially hostile social "outside." Eliot—like Davies—rejects open rebellion: Her protagonists' moral educations, then, of necessity lead them to renunciation. Subjectivity for Eliot is essentially interior, feminine, and defined by renunciation—that is to say, by the vision of domestic ideology rather than liberal individualism.

Most important, perhaps, for Eliot, the material effects of such a conception of subjectivity did not necessarily appear to be loss or failure. In her skeptical view, and perhaps in her experience, exclusion from corporate institutions—such as the university—represented more possibilities for the development of authentic selves than inclusion in their moribund and/or commodified projects. Both fulfilling family ties, whose abstract moral significance she emphasized, and corporate life are largely absent from the lives of her heroines (Dorothea, for example, is an orphan, with an ineffectual guardian; her own maternity is practically a footnote)—also true of Eliot herself, autodidact and, for some time, social pariah. The frequent complaint that Eliot withheld from her heroines her own moral and intellectual triumphs ignores the similarities among them. Eliot, like her heroines, remained excluded from institutional and corporate intellectual projects and came to glorify that exclusion; the two intellectual positions that are celebrated in *Middlemarch,* that of the intellectual/romantic alliance (Dorothea and Will) and that of the autodidact (Mary Garth), are those around which she constructed her personal and authorial identity, as "Mrs. Lewes" and as "George Eliot."

Chapter 5

"Strange [in]difference of sex"
Thomas Hardy and the Temptations of Androgyny

By the time of Thomas Hardy's death in 1928, this son of a provincial stonemason had survived two literary careers—one as a celebrated novelist, and one as a tolerated poet—to become a living legend. His ashes were interred in Poets' Corner in Westminster Abbey, a distinction that the equally magisterial Eliot, who died in 1880, had desired and failed to achieve. "George Eliot is known not only as a great writer, but as a person whose life and opinions were in notorious antagonism to Christian practice in regard to marriage, and Christian theory in regard to dogma," wrote T. H. Huxley (qtd. in Haight, 548–49), pointing out that a house of Christian worship could not reasonably be asked to shepherd heterodoxy to its eternal rest. Hardy certainly expressed more openly hostile opinions about both marriage and Christian dogma than Eliot's novels ever did, but he did not personally flout marriage law. In the forty-eight years that separated the deaths of these two Victorian novelists, literary conventions governing the representation of sex and gender conflict had changed dramatically, and Hardy himself had done as much as any novelist to change them.

From the 1840s through the 1870s, as we have seen in the works of Brontë, Eliot, and Leonowens, narratives of women's intellectual aspiration channeled that aspiration, with varying degrees of success, through plots of romance and marriage. The authors of narratives of female intellectual ambition were generally women; their protagonists never expressed overtly sexual aspirations; and although characters and authors might raise questions about the position of women, they rarely advocated specific responses. In the last third of the century, however, as women began to make real incursions into areas of culture—higher education, the professions—that had been male preserves, cultural discourses of control over women became more explicitly embodied and sexualized.

The early Victorian discourse of Woman had been couched in the metaphorical vocabularies of literature, religion, and philosophy; the domestic angel who was the subject of debate through the 1870s remained a largely incorporeal figure. She grew more substantial as actual middle-class women began to demand first social privileges (access to elite forms and institutions of education; employment in the professions) and then political ones (the suffrage). By the 1870s, when colleges for women had been established at both Oxford and Cambridge, it was apparent that the wall of educational disability keeping middle-class women from the exercise of civic and economic power was bound to fall. At that time, the protoscientific theorizing about women and gender difference of such philosophers as Auguste Comte and Herbert Spencer, emphasizing the separate and specialized roles of women as mothers and nurturers of the race, was joined by more assertively empirical accounts of sexual differentiation such as Darwin's *Descent of Man, and Selection in Relation to Sex* (1871).[1] Evolutionary theory influenced the medical domains of psychiatry and gynecology, which increased their descriptive and prescriptive power over women, in what it is tempting to regard as a direct response to women's encroachments into education, politics, and the regulation of sexual morality. Opponents of the higher education movement, for example, began to argue that intellectual overstimulation was fatal to women's reproductive capacities and that social investment in educational institutions for women constituted a form of race suicide.

This new, more embodied discourse of female insurgency found fictional embodiment in the "New Woman," a female protagonist who often balked at marriage law, the sexual double standard, and masculine sexuality in general. This protagonist appeared not only in novels by women, such as Sarah Grand and George Egerton (Mary Chavelita Dunne), but also in the work of male novelists such as Thomas Hardy and George Gissing. Of course male Victorian novelists had created insurgent female protagonists previously—although they tended, like Thackeray's Becky Sharp, to be positioned as antiheroines. Hardy's heroines are different: these female protagonists represent their creator's —that is, masculine—ambitions. Once the fictional heroine has been sexualized, her social insurgency, and in particular her intellectual ambition, makes her a plausible representative for the intellectual ambition of socially marginalized *male* intellectuals, such as Hardy. In this chapter, I argue that Hardy's depiction of negotiations between male and female protagonists over sexual and intellectual aspirations in the early novel, *A Pair of Blue Eyes* (1873), and his final novel, *Jude the Obscure* (1896), reveals the evolution of an androgynous ideal of intellectual ambition and fulfillment.

The notoriously macabre details of Hardy's interment dramatize a persistent division in his identity as a self-made man of letters. Fellow literary men J. M. Barrie and Sydney Cockerell quickly arranged for the Westminster Abbey ceremony, but Hardy's own instructions and the feelings of his family directed that he be laid in the churchyard at Stinsford, the parish of his birth, with his parents, grandparents, and first wife. The compromise reached was that his heart should be removed from his body and buried at Stinsford and the rest of him cremated and placed in Westminster Abbey. This queasy division of the spoils epitomizes the conflict between origins and attainments that haunted Hardy throughout his career. The struggle between his widow, Florence Dugdale Hardy, and Sydney Cockerell, first over his physical and then over his literary remains, inflects that division with a further distinction of gender.[2] Florence Hardy seems to embody the claims of domesticity and kinship, while Cockerell and Barrie represent a masculine public literary eminence. This schema tellingly links femininity to the foregone realm of origins, masculinity to the triumphant realm of becoming, but it does not fully capture the complexity of the gender and class identifications of the self-made man of letters whose position Hardy exemplifies.

A conventionally Victorian conflict between the domestic and social

demands of women and the intellectual development of the male protagonist does recur in Hardy's novels; for example, *Jude the Obscure*
imagines as one explanation for Jude's failure the financial, sexual, and
emotional claims made on him by Arabella and Sue: "Strange that his
first aspiration towards academical proficiency had been checked by a
woman, and that his second aspiration—towards apostleship—had also
been checked by a woman," Jude muses (228). But intellectual leanings
are not restricted to Hardy's male protagonists: Elfride Swancourt in *A
Pair of Blue Eyes* and the eponymous heroine of *The Hand of Ethelberta*
(1875) are both storytellers; other Hardy heroines, including Bathsheba
Everdene, Grace Melbury, and Sue Bridehead, have educational attainments that set them apart from, and have the potential to raise them
above, their immediate surroundings. Indeed, specifically artistic and
aesthetic impulses—Ethelberta's storytelling, Elfride's novel, Felice
Charmond's brief acting career in *The Woodlanders* (1887)—are generally associated with women.

The circumstances of Hardy's own career suggest that these heroines represent not an antithesis to the ambitions of the author but an expression of them. The autobiographical *Life of Thomas Hardy* (1928),
with its evasiveness about Hardy's antecedents and thorough chroni-
cling of his later society connections, reveals that Hardy's own literary
aspirations were embedded as much in the social restlessness of Eustacia Vye or Grace Melbury as in the reforming intellectual zeal of Clym
Yeobright or Angel Clare. Hardy's position resembles that of his heroines to the extent that their intellectual development often becomes the
means of improving their social standing. Unlike his heroine, Hardy
had for the achievement of his ambitions social and financial, as well as
intellectual, vehicles other than the traditionally feminine one of pru-
dent marriage. His assault on the fiction market after his first marriage
is a reminder that the image of the novelist as engaged primarily in self-
expression, and only latterly in professional negotiation, has always
been an idealization of a profession whose relationship to profit was
covert almost from its inception.[3] As Peter Widdowson writes, "Hardy,
in deciding to become a writer, had a careful eye on the market and its
requirements. This is borne out by his response to the earliest criticisms
from publishers' readers, editors, and reviewers of his first works"
(134). In the pursuit of publication, Hardy was willing to alter plot elements and prose to placate nervous journal editors, and he was typical

rather than exceptional in his attention—shared by Charles Dickens and George Eliot, among others—to the financial details of publication, reproduction, and copyright.

Hardy's oblique identification with the ambitions of his heroines is not idiosyncratic but revealing of the feminized structure of the literary marketplace and particularly the production of fiction. The novel was considered the most feminized Victorian literary genre, partly because of its alleged intellectual informality. George Eliot's midcentury pronouncement is typical: "No educational restrictions can shut women out from the materials of fiction, and there is no species of art which is so free from rigid requirements" (*Selected Essays,* 162). Whether or not this openness actually existed, the emphasis on the femininity of fiction obscured the fact that it was not only women of all classes who were excluded by their gender from the elite institutions (public schools and universities) that controlled access to cultural capital and authority: men of the working and lower middle classes suffered "educational restrictions" too. As Mary Poovey writes: "Even though literacy was increasingly available to members of the lower classes, access to the world of professional letters was still determined in the first instance by one's ability to write in a certain way, with an acceptable breadth of allusion, and according to recognized paradigms, genres and modes of address" (107). That access was determined by both class and gender. Once the man of letters achieved some success, however, an antecedent exclusion from elite institutions might be ideologically recuperated as a benign seclusion. Like the discourse of separate spheres that apotheosized the domestic angel as above the capitalist fray, "literary discourse . . . acquir[ed] its moral authority by its (putative) distance from the 'masculine' sphere of alienation and market relations" (Poovey, 125).[4] The price of this recuperation was thus the borrowing of a feminine model, and to some extent, a devaluation of the very activity—novel writing—being redeemed. That devaluation, partly a consequence of feminization, no doubt contributed to the disdain that Hardy always expressed for his novel-writing career, and his insistence that poetry was his true métier.

Social advancement subjected the successful man of letters to another feminizing structure. Although the designation of genius might be under the control of a largely male literary elite, it was women who conferred the respectability and status without which genius could not be fully publicized and enjoyed. "Cultivated" society was putatively a sphere of female power, whose norms were determined by feminine sensibility and judgments and administered by upper-class women. A nostalgic novelistic tradition—in evidence, for example, in *Great Expectations*—suspects upward mobility as emasculating in itself, representing working-class masculinity as more virile, because subject to physical and material, rather than mental and emotional laws, than its upper-class counterpart. (The same tradition, of course, codes working-class femininity as deficient: even cleaned up and elevated from drudge to domestic influence, Biddy, in *Great Expectations,* remains unacceptable for Pip.) Unfortunately for the working-class hero, intellectual and social achievement can be registered fully only within a sphere defined not only by its distance from physical labor but also by the prominence of feminine judgments codified as domesticity in the middle class, and "society" among the elite. From Dickens to Hardy to Lawrence and beyond, therefore, the aspiring male protagonist who is educated out of his provincial, working-class background suffers the loss of his original conceptions of masculine identity and social reality. No longer able to share the masculinity of his father—the blacksmith, the builder, the coal miner—he must find new standards for the creation of his adult masculine identity. One such standard is the ability to attract women of observable social and intellectual worth (Estella for Pip; Elfride for Stephen Smith; Ursula Brangwen for Rupert Birkin) over whom the male protagonist attempts to display his new dominance, but whose own social preeminence is, at the same time, the sign of his arrival.

If we consider Dickens the exemplary Victorian male novelist, Lawrence the representative Modern, and Hardy the hinge of late-Victorian/proto-Modern sensibility, it is not surprising that Hardy's representation of the anxiety of feminization at the heart of Victorian intellectual masculinity is the most divided. The suspicion of the feminine exemplified in *A Pair of Blue Eyes* gives way to the temptation of androgyny in *Jude the Obscure.* In *A Pair of Blue Eyes,* the attraction between the literarily inclined, working-class male protagonist and the clever, middle-class heroine eventuates in her death and is rerouted into an alliance between the hero and an older, middle-class man whose values he shares; the novel is partly structured by the misogyny of what Eve Kosofsky Sedgwick has termed "male homosocial desire." In *Jude the Obscure,* an attraction between Jude Fawley, of similarly humble antecedents, and Sue Bridehead, somewhat arbitrarily rendered as possessing middle-class, feminine refinement, also suggests that heterosexual alliances, particularly across real or apparent class lines, are fatal. *Jude the Obscure,* however, is much more reflective than the earlier novel in its estimation of the shaping pressure of gender on intellectual aspiration. In its lack of interest in masculine solidarity, its insistence on the similarities between its male and female protagonists, and, most important, its tentative exploration of the attractions of androgyny, *Jude the Obscure* is the most radical as well as the most pessimistic of Hardy's novels. The excessive and finally irresolute force of Hardy's representations of gender conflict illuminates a more general late-Victorian struggle to construct an acceptably masculine literary persona.

This struggle simultaneously articulates with and resists the contemporaneous struggle of middle-class women to construct an acceptably feminine intellectual ambition. For Hardy's women as for his men, however intellectual ambition is also always social. Peter Widdowson takes an optimistic view of the outcome of these struggles for Hardy's female protagonists: "At the heart . . . of Hardy's displaced class are women with greater potential for upward social mobility than men—or, to put it another way, for emancipation from the constraints of a disabling class society predicated on patriarchy" (215). But Hardy's heroines' upward mobility tends to end in loss: Elfride Swancourt dies, Sue Bridehead reenters a loveless marriage. Rather than point the way to emancipation from patriarchy, Hardy's female protagonists, like his heroes, seem to register the costs not only of emancipation to both genders but also of gender division itself to the subjects it divides. Indeed, if Hardy, despite the frequent misogyny of his narrative voice and the punitive outcomes of his plots, remains a compelling figure for feminist criticism, it is precisely because of his recognition of the Pyrrhic quality, and frequent failure, of patriarchal resolutions. At the same time, he remains unable fully to imagine the emancipation toward which both his heroines and his heroes strive.

A Pair of Blue Eyes is partly a *jeu d'esprit* along the lines of those of Hardy's poems that he later designated as "Satires of Circumstance," an ironical but pastoral quadrille. Its rigid formal structure is matched by a stark division between male friendship and mentorship, on the one hand, and heterosexual attraction and romantic love, on the other. The plot turns on the class difference between Stephen Smith, a young, self-educated architectural clerk who is the son of a master mason and a dairywoman, and Elfride Swancourt, the daughter of a snobbish rector, who sings prettily, rides well, and often writes her father's sermons. Elfride is conscious of the charm of her accomplishments, but her geographical and social isolation keeps her in ignorance of their precise value in the marketplace of social aspiration. When Stephen is dispatched by his employer to Swancourt's parish to restore the church, he and Elfride fall in love, encouraged by Swancourt, who does not know that Stephen's parents are among the lower ranks of his own parishioners. On Swancourt's outraged discovery of the facts, the lovers attempt to elope, but Elfride gets cold feet, and Stephen goes to work in India while she promises to wait for his professional success to amend his antecedents. Meanwhile, Elfride writes and publishes, anonymously, a medieval romance that is reviewed, anonymously (and scathingly), by Henry Knight, a man of letters who has been Stephen's mentor. Knight and Elfride become acquainted; he makes light of Elfride's ambitions. With a masochism that Hardy seems to regard as natural in women, she falls in love with him and abandons her secret engagement to the more thoroughly admiring Stephen. The triangle ends tragically, as Stephen, upon his return, silently yields Elfride to Knight, who discovers the history of the abortive elopement and casts her off. Despairing, she marries the local lord of the manor, miscarries, and dies. Stephen and Knight, each of whom has independently decided to ask for her hand again, find themselves on the same train to what turns out to be her funeral; having arrived as bitter rivals, they depart united in grief.

Intellectual ambition here has different consequences for the female protagonist than for the men. Elfride's intellectual pretensions—by bringing her within the ambit of Henry Knight's literary world and making him an object of admiration to her—expose her to sexual scandal, a connection Hardy frequently makes. In *The Return of the Native* (1878), for example, Eustacia Vye's father, after inveighing against modern education, is asked whether "Miss Eustacia had as much in her head that comes from books as anybody about here?" and responds presciently, "Perhaps if Miss Eustacia, too, had less romantic nonsense in her head it would be better for her" (107). Similarly, in *The Woodlanders,* a boarding-school education causes Grace Melbury to reject her faithful suitor, the woodcutter Giles Winterbourne, and marry the faithless Dr. Fitzpiers. Women's intellectual ambition subjects them to male sexual predation, often with tragic consequences (both Eustacia Vye and Giles Winterbourne end up dead).

Men's intellectual ambitions also lead them into conflict with women but through more complicated routes. In *A Pair of Blue Eyes,* the mentor/ephebe relationship between Stephen and Knight conflicts from the outset with the romance between Stephen and Elfride. When Stephen first mentions Knight to Elfride, she protests, "I don't care how good he is; I don't want to know him, because he comes between me and you. . . . When you are thinking of him I am shut out of your mind" (64). Although the possession of an accomplished woman is a sign of class status for the man, only men can act as role models for intellectual advancement. "'I shall try to become [Knight's] intimate friend some day,'" Stephen tells Elfride, "'he originally came from the same place as I, and taught me things; but I am not intimate with him. Shan't I be glad when I get richer and better known, and hob and nob with him!' Stephen's eye sparkled" (64). It is difficult to tell whether intellectual, social, or even romantic aspirations put the sparkle in Stephen's eye. But without distinguishing among these possibilities, Elfride intuits that male mentorship provides an alternative to heterosexual relations, a funnel for ambition that bypasses her altogether.

The notion that the companionship of women—even, or perhaps especially, intelligent ones—threatened the communal retention of male privilege found its ideological application in the latter part of the nineteenth century in the debate over the higher education of women. In her study of women novelists of Somerville College, Susan Leonardi identifies fear as the prime motivation for nineteenth-century opposition to female students there: "[F]irst . . . that the character of Oxford as a haven for the intellectual life and a ground for the establishment of male relationships would be diluted by the presence of women; second, fears that women themselves would change in various ways to the detriment of men and society" (20). In a complementary analysis, Linda Dowling has demonstrated that the Victorian construction of masculinity at Oxford appropriated the language of "Hellenism," or identification with the Greek republican ideal, to give value to male homosexual desire and homosocial community. Using the Greek ideal to associate heterosexuality with effeminacy, this appropriation, in Dowling's brilliantly paradoxical account, also played on fears of social disintegration.

A Pair of Blue Eyes is not focused on institutional developments; for men of Stephen's background, the elite universities function as rumors rather than established features of the landscape. Nevertheless, the novel's model of male intellectual life is informed by that dominant ideological scheme, with its fear of the dilution of male relationships and "intellectual life" by the distraction of heterosexual desire. Hardy borrows from a Hellenistic vocabulary of masculine ardor, as when Stephen muses over the irony that "his rival should be Knight, whom once upon a time he had adored as a man is very rarely adored by another in modern times" (238). At the same time, however, Stephen Smith is not a member of the Oxford elite for whom homosocial community might enshrine real privileges. On the contrary, responding to his mother's suspicions of Elfride, he exclaims, "'Why, to marry her would be the great blessing of my life—socially and practically, as well as in other respects'" (89). But it is, of course, a sign of Stephen's relatively low-class status that marriage to a woman like Elfride can elevate it.

One of Hardy's letters gives some clue as to what a Stephen Smith (or a Jude Fawley) might find both appealing and threatening about raising himself through such a heterosexual alliance. Hardy complained to one his early female correspondents of "having been denied by circumstances until very lately the society of educated womankind, which teaches men what cannot be acquired from books, and is indeed the only antidote to that bearishness which one gets into who lives much alone" (Millgate, 149). The terms of this apparently self-denigrating compliment echo the passage from *Middlemarch* in which the infatuated and doomed Lydgate tells Rosamond Vincy: "An accomplished woman almost always knows more than we men, though her knowledge is of a different sort. I am sure you could teach me a thousand things—as an exquisite bird could teach a bear if there were any common language between them" (131). Eliot's deeply ironic formulation—Lydgate is later forced to reflect that "[Rosamond] no more identified herself with him than if they had been creatures of different species" (487)—makes plainer than Hardy's the compensatory structure and dangerous ignorance of such obeisances to feminine cultivation. Intended to foster the skills in women to palliate or complement masculine intellect without interfering with its privileges, the gendered distinction between accomplishments and the learning that is "acquired from books" establishes a hostile heterosexual economy that circulates opposing and unfulfillable desires.

The triangulated, rivalrous relations among Stephen, Elfride, and Knight partly exemplify the narrative structure of male homosociality identified by Sedgwick. In a defining moment of that structure, according to Sedgwick, masculine bonds are strengthened across class distinctions by the destruction of a woman. Central to this outcome is "the scene wherein male rivals unite, refreshed in mutual support and definition, over the ruined carcase of a woman. . . . The spectacle of the ruin of a woman . . . is just the right lubricant for an adjustment in differentials of power" between men (Sedgwick, 76). *A Pair of Blue Eyes* concludes, apparently, with such a moment, as Knight and Stephen, previously unable to respond to each other outside of a frame of condescension/adulation defined by their relative class positions and ages, "side by side . . . retrac[e] their steps down the grey still valley to Castle Boterel" (371). Yet the elegiac mood of this conclusion makes it difficult to see its protagonists as "refreshed"; and the scene before them emphasizes not only the ruin of Elfride but also the distance of both men from the class position of her aristocratic widower. The triangle in *A Pair of Blue Eyes,* in other words, points less to the recuperation than to the failure of masculinity—particularly intellectual masculinity—in its encounter with heterosexuality and the feminine.

Furthermore, the novel's triangle can be viewed as emblematic of individual psychology rather than social relations: that is, Stephen and Knight are younger and older, less and more successful, versions of the same self—united by their resemblance to their creator. Hardy claimed that if any character in *A Pair of Blue Eyes* was autobiographical, it was Henry Knight rather than Stephen Smith (*Life and Works of Thomas Hardy,* 76), but one might equally claim that the resemblance is divided between them: Stephen is the eager young architect's apprentice that Hardy was, Knight is the man of letters he might have imagined himself becoming. In this developmental model, male maturity depends on the nature of a man's relationship to a woman: homosocially directed desire is routed through heterosexual attraction even when its object is a projection of the self. Immature men, such as Stephen, are patronized by, feel inferior to, or actually are the social or intellectual inferiors of the women to whom they are attracted; mature, successful men naturalize that inferiority by reversing it.

In *A Pair of Blue Eyes,* however, no men actually attain such maturity. Both Stephen Smith and Henry Knight remain notably effeminate.

On first meeting Stephen, Elfride reports to her father: "His face is—well—*pretty;* just like mine'" (16). In a paragraph of tortured prose, we are told that Stephen shares with Elfride an "inflammable disposition": "Elfride's emotions were as sudden as his in kindling, but the least of woman's lesser infirmities—love of admiration—caused an inflammable disposition on his part, so exactly similar to her own, to appear as meritorious in him as modesty made her own seem culpable in her" (24). The sense of the passage is that Elfride approves of Stephen's responsiveness because it flatters her vanity; but the syntax emphasizes the identity between Stephen and Elfride ("so exactly similar to her own") and even, briefly, suggests that "woman's . . . infirmities" are being attributed to Stephen. Again, after the two reach an understanding, Elfride tells Stephen she loves him "because [he is] so docile and gentle." Stephen is conscious that something is amiss in Elfride's motives: "'Those are not quite the correct qualities for a man to be loved for,' said Stephen, in a rather dissatisfied tone of self-criticism" (63). Hardy himself seems ambivalent about not only his hero's possession of feminine qualities but also their significance:

> [Stephen's] constitution was made up of very simple particulars; was one which, rare in the springtime of civilizations, seems to grow abundant as a nation gets older, individuality fades, and education spreads; that is, his brain had extraordinary receptive powers, and no great creativeness. Quickly acquiring any kind of knowledge he saw around him, and having a plastic adaptability more common in woman than in man, he changed colour like a chameleon as the society he found himself in assumed a higher and more artificial tone. (92–93)

In this Darwinian model, in which the evolution of the species appears simultaneously as its entropic degeneration, progress up the social ladder from physical to mental labor is not necessarily amenable to traditionally masculine methods (forcible or adversarial) of self-advancement but may call upon the dubious skills—artifice, adaptability—by which women, in the history of the novel, at least, more frequently rise. This suggestion that the future is effete, indeed feminine, is frequent in Hardy, so that in *Tess of the D'Urbervilles,* for example, it is Tess whose personal melancholy represents "feelings that might almost have been called those of the age—the ache of modernism" (105).

The transfer of Elfride's affections to Henry Knight, however, and the resulting narrative attention to him, raises the possibility that Stephen's effeminacy may be a function of his youth, rather than his constitution or embodiment of an effete civilization. In Stephen's eyes, certainly, Knight represents a more virile model of the man of letters, particularly because he is not associated with the production of fiction. To Elfride's query, "Is [Knight] only a reviewer?" Stephen replies with ardent pomposity that his position is "finer than being a novelist considerably. . . . He really is a literary man of some eminence. . . . He writes things of a higher class than reviews. . . . His ordinary productions are social and ethical essays" (64). But Hardy does not share Stephen's naïveté: If he identified with Knight, then the debacle of Knight's romantic career (that shatters, at least temporarily, his literary one) has the character of a self-admonishment. Hardy speculates that Knight is a "bachelor by nature" (186) and rapidly demonstrates that Stephen and Knight himself are mistaken in conflating intellectual achievement with virility. Knight's pose of man of the world cannot stand up to an actual heterosexual encounter. Elfride's charms play upon an "imagination . . . fed up to a preternatural size by lonely study and silent observation of his kind—[and] emotions . . . drawn out long and delicate by his seclusion, like plants in a cellar," while "several years of poetic study, and, if the truth must be told, poetic efforts, had tended to develope [sic] the affective side of his constitution still further, in proportion to his active faculties" (298). In other words, like a woman (and like Stephen), Knight is sensitive, receptive, and imaginative. He is also less sexually experienced than Elfride, who has been kissed before, so that at the moment when he seems to have arrived at the certainty of masculine triumph, he can experience only its humiliating absence: "How childishly blind he must have seemed to this mere girl! How she must have laughed at him inwardly!" (297). Knight is wrong in imagining that Elfride has been mocking him for his lack of experience—she has, indeed, symmetrically been fearing his discovery of her inappropriate possession of it—but his extreme reaction demonstrates the tenuousness of his sense of superiority to, and difference from, the feminine.

The idea of mature masculinity as—tenuously—invested in the ability to demonstrate intellectual and sexual superiority to women whose social superiority gives the demonstration significance marks not only Hardy's novels but also the progress of his career, which is punctuated by relationships with literarily inclined women of varied class backgrounds. These begin with the middle-class respectability of his first wife, Emma Gifford (like Elfride Swancourt, a rector's daughter), attain a social peak in his friendship with intellectually active socialites such as Florence Henniker and Agnes Grove, and culminate in his marriage to Florence Dugdale, whose antecedents and ambitions closely resembled his own. That final marriage might seem socially anticlimactic in Hardy's long rise to intellectual eminence, but Hardy's marriages and his society friendships represent two distinct models of negotiating sexual, social, and intellectual standing across gender.

Both sets of relationships are structured by a tension between reciprocity and disavowal. The marriages, at least at the outset, seem to have been imagined as working partnerships, in which both partners invested their ambitions and abilities in a single product—Hardy's intellect. Robert Gittings describes the joint educational effort early in Hardy's first marriage:

> Under Hardy's direction, [Emma Hardy] had set herself to copy into a stout ruled notebook the extracts from books and newspaper he had made in previous years, and to bring them up to date with quotations from his recent reading. The raw material for a self-taught and self-improving novelist was laid out neatly in her still-schoolgirl hand, and by the beginning of April 1876, she had provided him with over 200 entries. . . . Emma's labour was clearly designed to provide fodder for his future productions. (2)

Florence Dugdale, whom Hardy married after his career as a novelist had ended, served as his amanuensis in a more direct project of self-making. She had been a journalist and children's book author: after the marriage, her greatest literary contribution was the hoax of the autobiographical *Life and Works of Thomas Hardy*, written in the third person by Hardy, collated and typed by Florence, and published under her name. This fiction, which might seem to publicize Florence Hardy as a writer, paradoxically serves to obscure her: although the name is hers, the voice that it circulates is his. The *Life and Works of Thomas Hardy* simultaneously advertises the feminine, in its attribution and its celebration of Hardy's connections with society women; exploits it, in the harnessing of Florence's name and labor; and erases it, in its reticence about both Florence and Emma.

Hardy's literary career, then, can be viewed as the single product of triple labor and ambitions. Because there is no evidence that either Emma or Florence Hardy possessed great literary talent, the allocation of resources was no doubt efficient, but it was also clearly determined by, and representative of, prevailing gender arrangements. The marriage of Jane Welsh and Thomas Carlyle, for example, displays a similar structure, including the subsuming of Jane's literary ambitions, the division caused by Carlyle's attraction to the society hostess Lady Harriet Ashburton, and his regret for his neglect after Jane's death.[5] In their self-representation as men of letters, Hardy and Carlyle typify a complex pattern, disavowing the feminizing labor and ambition in which their middle-class wives had participated, and which they had witnessed and employed, but displaying associations with upper-class women as signs of their achievement.

If Hardy's relationships with socially powerful women subsumed them less, they nevertheless suggest a functionalist and formalized model of heterosexual reciprocity. Florence Henniker, for example, the daughter of Lord Houghton, who was "from her earliest years . . . accustomed to high society, cosmopolitan and literary" (Gittings, 72), was not dependent on Hardy for the fulfillment of her own aspirations, as were his wives. But if society women's attentions to Hardy assured and signified his achievement, his attentions to them could ratify their intellectual claims. This reciprocal structure is static, a minuet in which each partner must perform a single step, male intellect guiding female accomplishment, female accomplishment enhancing male intellect. The structure remains in place even when the content suggests its insufficiency. When Hardy met Henniker in 1893, she had already published three novels; Hardy nevertheless approached her as raw material, offering himself as her literary mentor. He collaborated with her on a short story, edited her prose, advised her on publication, and wrote to agents and publishers on her behalf. "Speaking very generally," he wrote to her, "I think you are not likely to be treated very badly: one reason is that you being a friend of mine would make a publisher remember that you are likely to know the tricks of the trade." Similarly, he wrote to her in 1896: "Many thanks for your little 'Brand of Discord' which I have read, and like everything about except the title. It is as good as anything you have done, and resembles rather the work of an experienced writer than of a novice" (Hardy and Pinion, 32, 58). In that same year, Henniker was elected president of the Society of Women Journalists.

Henniker may indeed have benefited from Hardy's greater fame, experience, and aesthetic judgment; nevertheless, he seems as much to be constructing a fantasy of a woman in need of his mentorship as assisting one who actually was. J. M. Barrie wrote after Hardy's death: "I have read the letters to Mrs. Henniker. . . . I rather grudge her being a writer at all, and indeed I believe Hardy did also. . . . She was delightful and cultured and could take him on holiday from himself (for which I bless her)" (qtd. in Hardy and Pinion, xxxvii). Considering the degree to which Hardy strove to aid Henniker in her literary career, we might conclude that Barrie, as he half admits, is simply projecting his own unselfconsciously "grudging" response to female intellect. But the diminutives Hardy consistently applied to Henniker's work ("your little 'Brand of Discord'") and his condescension accord with Barrie's interpretation. Florence Hardy, as well, divined a similar unspoken resentment of her writing: "I have a feeling deep within me," she wrote, "'that my husband rather dislikes my being a scribbling woman'" (qtd. in Gittings, 161). Hardy's interest in Henniker's work provides an occasion for him to demonstrate his intellectual superiority in a relationship whose social benefits were conferred by her.

The preceding analysis suggests that although, on the one hand, the masculinity of the man of letters is threatened by his proximity to the position of the middle-class woman in exclusion from institutionalized norms of education and knowledge, on the other, he is dependent upon women both for practical aid and for the ratification of his social standing. In this context, heterosexual reciprocity is always also a kind of competition, because it is based on the granting or withholding of social and intellectual, as well as (or under cover of) sexual, favors. Where early and mid-Victorian women writers such as Brontë, Eliot, and Leonowens downplayed the sexual exchange implicit in such negotiations, in the novels of Hardy and other late-Victorian writers associated with the "New Woman," this sexual aspect of the exchange becomes more and more explicit, although social and intellectual negotiations retain their importance. In *Jude the Obscure,* Hardy revisits the quadrilateral structure of a mentor/ephebe relationship on the one hand, and a romantic entanglement on the other, that I have outlined in my discussion of *A Pair of Blue Eyes*. In this last novel, however, the neat division of these relationships along gender lines becomes disarranged. While Jude Fawley's relationship with Sue Bridehead is certainly represented as a dizzying succession of intellectual advances and sexual withdrawals on her part, *Jude the Obscure* nevertheless attempts to replace this combative reciprocity with something closer to mutuality or alliance: the lovers come close to being mentors as well.

The nineteenth-century reception of Hardy's novels exemplifies the condescension that a male author of his class and educational background might expect from reviewers. Victorian women writers, also excluded from elite educational institutions, were famously castigated for not conforming to expectations that they would write about emotional or romantic situations, rather than intellectual or political ideas. But women were by no means alone in being patronized or dictated to about their proper style and subject matter. Even as Hardy became the pre-eminent living English novelist, reviewers continued to object to his choices of vocabulary and setting when they departed from the pastoral. However consciously or ironically he might take as a theme inequities of access to language and erudition, Hardy's tendency to put in the mouths of his characters the same range of allusions that he himself had acquired annoyed his critics and gave them frequent opportunities to put him in his place—which, they felt, was in the country. For example, the *Quarterly Review*'s reader, Mowbray Morris, pronounced of *Tess of the D'Urbervilles:*

> [Hardy] is too apt to affect a certain preciosity of phrase which has a somewhat incongruous effect in a tale of rustic life; he is too fond—and the practice has been growing on him through all his later books—of making experiments in a form of language which he does not seem clearly to understand, and in a style for which he was assuredly not born. It is a pity, for Mr. Hardy had a very good style of his own once, and one moreover excellently suited to the subjects he knew and was then content to deal with. (Lerner and Holmstrom, 86–87)

The *Fortnightly*'s reviewer, too, objected that Hardy "will make [Tess] talk sometimes as the author of *Far From the Madding Crowd* is often wont to write" (Lerner and Holmstrom, 87). The two objections are not identical: the first is that Hardy expresses himself incongruously, the second is that he makes his characters do so as well. But as the second criticism makes clear, they share the same foundation: rural, lower-class, and sometimes female speakers are grasping after "a style for which [they were] . . . not born"—they are, in other words, transgressing boundaries of class and (in Tess's case) gender. Perhaps accidentally, the criticism also points to the gender transgression in Hardy's authorial identification: despite his notorious specular objectification of Tess, they share that "ache of modernism" that incorporates both the ambition to transgress boundaries and the fear of their dissolution.

This standard criticism of Hardy's language, in fact, ignores the degree to which his explicit subject is the use of language and intellect as a means and sign of such transgression. Linguistic pedantry occurs with remarkable frequency in moments of flirtation or jockeying for position between male and female characters. Crucial moments in *The Woodlanders,* for example, display this structure. Grace Melbury, meeting the eligible Fitzpiers in the woods as she searches for a purse she has lost, invokes *Robinson Crusoe:* "Indeed, money is of little more use at Hintock than on Crusoe's island; there's hardly any way of spending it." Fitzpiers interrupts his speculation about who gave her the purse in order to pay her a pedantic compliment: "You unconsciously practice [the cardinal virtues], Miss Melbury. . . . According to Schleiermacher they are Self-control, Perseverance, Wisdom, and Love; and his is the best list that I know" (107–8). Here, the intention of the lovers seems to be merely to impress each other with their cultivation; but such exchanges can be more sinister. At the end of the novel, Fitzpiers, having married Grace and then been extravagantly unfaithful to her, attempts to win her back by persuading her that his feelings have matured:

> "It is a different kind of love altogether . . . Less passionate; more profound. . . . 'Love talks with better knowledge, and knowledge with dearer love.'"

> "That's out of *Measure for Measure,*" said [Grace] slily.

> "O yes—I meant it as a citation," blandly replied Fitzpiers. (256)

The adverbs—"blandly" and "slily"—suggest that the speakers are consciously using "citation" as a form of manipulation. Fitzpiers attempts to impress Grace with a relatively esoteric reference; when she recognizes its source, he must claim that he was intending not to impress her but simply to refer to a mutual fund of knowledge. In either case, he is under an imputation of rhetorical calculation not entirely consistent with the expression of unabashed admiration. Erudition, in other words, is a social and romantic weapon or medium of exchange, not simply a result or sign of "intellect."[6]

The reception of *Jude the Obscure,* though by no means unanimously negative, certainly occasioned some of the most spectacular attacks on both Hardy's narrative and his moral attitudes. In addition to criticizing its sexual frankness, reviewers on the whole found *Jude the Obscure* a markedly divided narrative, because they were unable (or unwilling) to recognize the similarities between Jude's situation and Sue's. "After you have read 'Jude the Obscure,'" wrote one reviewer, "your thoughts run in two separate channels cut by Mr. Hardy's two nearly separate purposes. Your opinion of the book will largely depend on which you regard as the main one. These purposes are wound in with the history of Jude and the history of Sue." Jude's story tends to be regarded as that of "a man of the people with the native instincts of the scholar" (Lerner and Holmstrom, 130); whereas in the words of Edmund Gosse, who finds that "the *vita sexualis* of Sue is the central interest of the book," her story is "a terrible study in pathology" (Lerner and Holmstrom, 120, 121).

These views simultaneously naturalize scholarly and sexual ambitions as inherent, rather than socially developed, aspects of identity, and divide them along conventional gender lines. In fact, *Jude the Obscure* challenges precisely such distinctions between character as socially contingent and character as inherently constituted as well as those between masculine and feminine identity and aspirations. If the novel is explicitly concerned with Jude's intellectual aspirations and their failure, it is equally explicitly concerned with Sue's intellect,[7] while, despite the fascination exerted by Sue's sexual peculiarities, it is Jude whose sexual appetite precipitates the tragic action. It is not clear whether Jude's failure to attain even the smallest of his academic and theological ambitions proceeds from social injustice (the lack of access to Oxford for those without money) or failings represented as constitutional (his weaknesses for women and liquor); he himself gestures toward both explanations

(344–45). Similarly, we can never be sure whether Sue owes her undoubted capriciousness to her individual constitution or to some flaw inherent in femininity itself: both possibilities are advanced at different times in the novel.[8]

As his preface to the 1912 Wessex edition of *Jude the Obscure* reveals, Hardy had mixed feelings about the novel's topical appeal and contribution to narratives of gender conflict and class struggle, as well as its protagonists' degree of representativeness. It is certainly the novel that most consistently and overtly represents its protagonists' struggle for, and self-conscious use of, a mastery of the culture of humane letters, but it is not narrowly autobiographical, any more than is Eliot's *Mill on the Floss*. For one thing, Hardy—like Eliot—withheld from his fictional characters his own successful mobility. It is, however, as the reader for the *Saturday Review* observed, "The first time in English literature [that] the almost intolerable difficulties that beset an ambitious man of the working class—the snares, the obstacles, the countless rejections and humiliations by which our society eludes the services of these volunteers—receive adequate treatment" (Lerner and Holmstrom, 136). In that sense it does give voice to the forming consciousness of a class to which its author certainly belonged, much as *Jane Eyre* was understood to give voice to a kind of female experience shared by its author. In both cases, reviewers read the novels through a cultural narrative that they then read back into the novel: just as Jane Eyre is hardly credible in the role of revolutionary "mouthpiece . . . to plead the cause of governesses" (Rigby, 176), so too Jude is an unlikely "ambitious man of the working class," with all the industrial, urban resonances that such a description would have had in the 1890s. His rattling of the gates of Christminster has a distinctly modern quality, but he is an artisan, a product of rural rather than urban disintegration.

Hardy, in any case, resisted his implication in the narrative of "intolerable difficulties," protesting perhaps too much against any connection between Jude's academic struggles and his own. In the *Life and Works of Thomas Hardy* he asserted that he "was not altogether hindered going [to university], at least to Cambridge, and could have gone up easily at five-and-twenty," and he gave a number of different reasons for his failure to do so (216, 296–97, 467). In the preface to *Jude the Obscure* he asserts that both the state of marriage law and the "difficulties down to twenty or thirty years back of acquiring knowledge in letters without pecuniary means" (xxxviii) were simply part of the story's "tragic machinery" (xxxvii); at the same time he notes, with a detach-ment behind which it is possible to detect some pride, that he "was in-formed that some readers thought . . . that when Ruskin College [for working men at Cambridge] was subsequently founded it should have been called the College of Jude the Obscure" (xxxviii). He similarly both asserts and distances himself from Sue's centrality as a contempo-rary type, coyly attributing to an unidentified "experienced reviewer of [Germany]" the opinion that "Sue Bridehead . . . was the first delin-eation in fiction of the . . . woman of the feminist movement—the slight, pale 'bachelor' girl—the intellectualized, emancipated bundle of nerves that modern conditions were producing, mainly in cities as yet" (xxxviii).

Yet it is not simply out of stubborn incomprehension that reviewers tended to focus on Hardy's representation of Sue's "pathological" sexu-ality. Although I will argue that he uses it to different ends, the vocabu-lary that Hardy finds for Sue's physical and emotional responses to her social situation is, like that of much "New Woman" fiction, clearly drawn from the contemporary scientific controversy over female intel-lect that I will call "gynecological antifeminism." The focus of reac-tionary anxiety was the specter of middle-class female power; the contemporaneous educational demands of working-class men—the me-chanics' institutes, working-men's colleges, and the university extension movement—failed to generate a similarly unified repressive discourse. Indeed, as the reception of *Jude the Obscure* suggests, the two large so-cial groups excluded from the educational advantages of middle- and upper-class men—men and women of the laboring classes and women of the middle and upper classes—rarely perceived themselves, and were rarely represented, as sharing either a class interest or a common sym-bolic significance within dominant culture. In *Jude the Obscure,* how-ever, intellectual and educational aspiration form the first link between the male and female protagonists. The novel participates ambivalently in the fin-de-siècle representation of the educated woman as mon-strously unsexed, representing that "pathology" as intensely attractive. At the same time, it reveals its hero as to some degree feminized and in-sists on the similitude between him and the heroine. Thus, although proposing no political alliance between the working-class man and the middle-class woman, the novel nevertheless attempts to rescue the androgynous intellect, figured in Sue Bridehead, from the discourse of gynecological antifeminism.

An exemplary text of that discourse, written by a psychiatrist in whose theories of degeneracy Hardy was interested (Dale, 207), is Henry Maudsley's "Sex in Mind and Education" (1874), published in the *Fortnightly Review*. Maudsley's fundamental concern is the propagation—or extinction—of the race. Scorning to palliate his argument by appeals to maternal instinct or rewards, he asserts that women's education must take into account "their peculiar functions and . . . their foreordained work as mothers and nurses of children. Whatever aspirations of an intellectual kind they may have, they cannot be relieved from the performance of those [maternal] offices so long as it is thought necessary that mankind should continue on earth" (471). According to Maudsley, the period of menarche that enables these "offices" is so physiologically stressful for women, and the recurrence of the "periodical functions" so disruptive, that the proper fulfillment of maternal duties is inconsistent with significant intellectual labor. Thus, women's intellectual aspirations are absolutely limited by the imperative to reproduce. When women ignore this imperative, the result is a monstrous androgyny that threatens humanity itself:

> It may be the plan of evolution to produce at some future period a race of sexless beings who, undistracted and unharassed by the ignoble troubles of reproduction, shall carry on the intellectual work of the world, not otherwise than as the sexless ants do the work and the fighting of the community. . . .
>
> Sex is fundamental, lies deeper than culture, cannot be ignored or defied with impunity. You may hide nature, but you cannot extinguish it. Consequently it does not seem impossible that if the attempt to do so be seriously and persistently made, the result may be a monstrosity—something which having ceased to be a woman is not yet a man—"*ce quelque chose de monstrueux,*" which the Comte A. de Gasparin forebodes, "*cet être repugnant, qui déja parait à notre horizon.*" (477–78)

Although Maudsley does not use the word "androgynous," the figure he envisions here—so terrifying as to be nameable only in French—

comports with the word's Victorian usage: "uniting the (physical) characters of both sexes, at once male and female" (*OED*). Maudsley imagines such a unity only in terms of loss and monstrosity, but his futurist pessimism certainly shares an imaginative universe with the Hardy of both the contemporaneous *A Pair of Blue Eyes* and the later *Jude the Obscure*. Stephen Smith's chameleonlike constitution, "rare in the springtime of civilization," implies a wintry, effete future; Sue reflects Maudsley's fears when she tells Jude: "Everybody is getting to feel as we do [about marriage]. We are a little beforehand, that's all. In fifty, a hundred, years the descendants of these two will . . . see weltering humanity still more vividly than we do now . . . and will be afraid to reproduce them" (301). But Hardy lacks Maudsley's monolithic conviction that the evolution of heterosexual relations can only signal degeneration. Perhaps because of his experience, as a man of letters, of gender ideology as both metastatic (lending its structure, for example, to the class position of the man of letters) and confining, Hardy in *Jude the Obscure* fitfully envisions the androgynous future as utopian. For example, Jude muses on his deathbed that he and Sue had ideas that "were fifty years too soon to be any good to us" (422–23), implying that those ideas might become more appropriate in some better future state. Furthermore, rather than invoke "Nature" to ratify the social status quo, as Maudsley does, Hardy represents the conflict of natural and social "law" as a human tragedy against whose effects both men and women must be expected to struggle.

If Hardy's portrait of Sue revises the image of female degeneracy that dominated the antifeminist discourse of the last quarter of the nineteenth century, it does so less by denying Maudsley's degenerative vision than by rewriting it as at least potentially evolutionary. Sue Bridehead's significant attraction for a number of the novel's male characters is, in fact, inseparable from her cerebral sexlessness. Hardy's representation of that appeal draws somewhat haphazardly on conflicting discourses of the feminine. A Hellenic aesthetic, recalling the homosocial structure of *A Pair of Blue Eyes,* appears in the celebration of Sue's eroticized boyishness at the expense of the blowsy female animal represented by Arabella: seeing Sue in his own suit, which she puts on after having walked through a river, Jude compares her with a "marine deity" and a "figur[e] in the Parthenon frieze" (149); she looks, to Jude's admiration, "boyish as a Ganymedes [*sic*]" (159). This boyishness, however, blends into an incorporeality itself open to conflicting interpretations. Sometimes the admiration of both the narrator and Jude of Sue as a "phantasmal, bodiless creature" (272) recalls the Victorian ideology of feminine passionlessness. "The average woman is in this superior to an average man—that she never instigates [sexual passion], only responds," Sue claims (372), echoing various Victorian dicta such as W. R. Greg's that in women, " the desire [for sex] is dormant, if not non-existent, till excited" (qtd. in Poovey, 5). Sometimes, on the other hand, her disembodiment seems not nostalgically ideal but proleptically degenerative, associated with her unusually developed intellect: "'My life has been entirely shaped by what people call a peculiarity in me,'" she explains, "'I have no fear of men, as such, nor of their books. I have mixed with them . . . almost as one of their own sex" (152). The confusion of representational strategies suggests that a vocabulary for celebrating the attractions of androgyny eludes Hardy. Nevertheless the coexistence in Sue of androgynous or even masculine traits with more conventionally feminine attractions emerges very clearly.

Visiting his aunt at Marygreen, Jude is presented with a series of verbal snapshots of the child Sue, first reciting poetry, "the smallest of them all, 'in her little white frock, and shoes, and pink sash'" (114) and then as "not exactly a tomboy, you know; but she could do things that only boys do, as a rule":

> "I've seen her hit in and steer down the long slide on yonder pond, with her little curls blowing. . . . All boys except herself. . . . "

> These retrospective visions of Sue only made Jude the more miserable that he was unable to woo her, and he left the cottage of his aunt that day with a heavy heart. He would fain have glanced into the school to see the room in which Sue's little figure had so glorified itself; but he checked his desire and went on. (115)

"Not exactly a tomboy," Sue is nevertheless able to "do things that only boys do," whether sliding on the ice or reading advanced literature; and it is the combination of that capacity with her feminine "white frock," "little curls," and "little figure" that renders her so desirable. Sue herself is conscious of the appeal of her unconventional combination of gender attributes: Hardy often represents her as attempting to control male demands through piquant demonstrations of erudition. "'Say those pretty lines, then, from Shelley's 'Epipsychidion' as if they meant me!' she solicited, slanting up closer to [Jude] as they stood. 'Don't you know them?' 'I know hardly any poetry,' he replied mournfully" (257). Sue has just annoyed Jude by informing him that she intends their elopement to be celibate; Hardy's choice of verbs—"solicited" and "slanting"—and Sue's pointed question suggest that her behavior is consciously both sexually stimulating and intellectually diminishing to her partner, who indeed responds to being thus put in his place with a resigned obedience to her wishes. On another occasion, informing Phillotson that she wishes to leave him for Jude, Sue quotes John Stuart Mill in support of her plan, leading her beleaguered husband to exclaim, "What do I care about J. S. Mill! I only want to lead a quiet life!" (286) In the first instance, Sue's literary knowledge gives her an advantage over Jude that operates as a class advantage; she is the refined lady, he the rustic clown, the "bearish" subject "denied by circumstances . . . the society of educated womankind," to quote again from Hardy's letter (Millgate, 149). In the second instance, an ability—however ludicrous it may seem—to move fluidly between ideas and emotions gives her an advantage over Phillotson, who is finally persuaded by the combination of emotional appeal and intellectual argument.

Despite the strained quality of the discussion between Sue and Phillotson, such metaphysical exchanges appear less anomalous in this novel than elsewhere, precisely because the inseparability of emotional and intellectual aspiration is the novel's actual subject. When Sue, having impulsively run away from her training college, spends the night in Jude's lodgings, dressed in his clothing, they flirt uneasily:

> "You called me a creature of civilization, or something, didn't you?" she said, breaking a silence. "It was very odd you should have done that."
>
> "Why?"

"Well, because it is provokingly wrong. I am a sort of negation of it."

"You are very philosophical. 'A negation' is profound talking."

"Is it? Do I strike you as being learned?" she asked, with a touch of raillery. (201)

Unlike the sparring of Grace and Fitzpiers in *The Woodlanders,* the exchange has a rhythm of natural banter appropriate to the situation of an unconventional female student and an intellectually ambitious artisan who, isolated by their aspirations, unexpectedly discover in each other kindred spirits.

Sue's manipulation of gender attributes, however, coexists with its opposite: a disdain for the hostile reciprocations of conventional heterosexuality. Jude finds what he terms her "epicene tenderness . . . harrowing" but reflects: "If he could only get over the sense of her sex, as she seemed to be able to do so easily of his, what a comrade she would make. She was nearer to him than any other woman he had ever met" (159). This proximity, or similarity, is emphasized throughout the novel. There is, it is true, a submerged class contrast in their relationship, which, if carried through the novel, would make Sue merely the emblem and prize of Jude's ambition. Although her actual origins are no more exalted than his, she is refined and urbane in contrast to Jude: "She was a long way removed from the rusticity that was his," he thinks on his first view of her (90). But this antithesis is overwhelmed by the novel's emphasis on their likeness, which everyone perceives. "What counterparts they were!" Jude reflects when Sue comes to him for refuge (149). They are soon able to read each other's thoughts: "When they talked on an indifferent subject . . . there was ever a second silent conversation passing between their emotions, so perfect was the reciprocity between them." Phillotson, explaining why he is condoning his wife's elopement with Jude, says, "I found from their manner that an extraordinary affinity, or sympathy, entered into their attachment . . . . Their supreme desire is to be together—to share each other's emotions, and fancies, and dreams" (242–43). Penny Boumelha has demonstrated that their lives follow very similar patterns (14–42), and Elizabeth Langland argues: "Through kinship and twinship with Sue, Jude seeks an alternative to the frustrating constructions of masculinity that his culture holds out" (Higonnet, ed., 33).

If he seek such an alternative, however, Jude does not achieve it: the ability to combine masculine and feminine traits is contained within Sue. Hardy seems to imply that women are more able to achieve and maintain an androgynous ideal partly for that most Victorian of reasons—their lesser sexual impulses. Jude, on the other hand, always finds Sue's sexless androgyny painful as well as attractive. Furthermore, despite their likeness, Jude's gender makeup is more static. He does display susceptibilities to the harshness of country life that are inappropriate to both his gender and his country origins. He feels sorry for animals: he makes common cause with the crows that he is supposed, as a young boy, to be scaring away, and after his marriage to Arabella, his inability to kill a pig properly causes her to call him a "tender-hearted fool." Although Jude also feels "dissatisfied with himself as a man at what he had done" (65), the cause of his dissatisfaction is not that he has done a bad job of killing the pig but that he has done it at all. He owes part of this susceptibility to the early advice of Phillotson to "be kind to animals and birds, and read all you can" (4–5), and Phillotson is a man of uncertain virility, particularly in his sexual relations. The young Jude also, like Henry Knight, has an emotional relationship to the classics he studies as he drives the baker's cart, impulsively kneeling one moonlit night to recite a poem of Horace to Diana. But if Jude seems feminized in the context of the relatively natural surroundings of Marygreen, such references drop off after he leaves for Christminster, where the emphasis is on his rough rusticity in contrast to what he imagines as Christminster refinement. In both contexts, however, the narrator portrays Jude (in contrast, for example, to Phillotson) as essentially masculine: in Marygreen, he is masculine culture to Arabella's voracious female nature; in Christminster, he is the masculine breadwinner in contrast to Sue's intermittent efforts to sustain their household.

Sue and Jude are not entirely cut off from the institutional resources of their class and era: Sue passes a scholarship exam and enters the Teacher's Training College at Melchester (which will qualify her for the career pursued by both of Hardy's sisters), and Jude attends public lectures and is briefly the leading light of the "Artizans' Mutual Improvement Society." But Sue runs away from her college when she is placed in solitary confinement after being out all night with Jude; Jude is forced to resign from the Mutual Improvement Society's committee when the irregularity of his marital status becomes known. The novel demonstrates the insufficiency of such institutions, which appear to offer their constituents opportunities for intellectual development but in fact operate as conduits for dominant class and gender ideologies, enforcing the most conventional standards of respectability and sexual division.

Jude the Obscure's fantasy of androgyny, then, embodied more fully in its female than in its male protagonist, does not fully erase the "sense of sex." The novel reveals that it is easier for Hardy to imagine the dissolution of gender than of class boundaries, and to do so by challenging the conventions of femininity rather than those of masculinity. No fantasy of classlessness parallels the yearning for androgyny; the class conflict incipient in Jude's ambition to matriculate at Christminster is subsumed, in the tradition of the domestic novel, by the novel's warped but recognizable marriage plot: social and intellectual conflicts become conflicts, conventionally, over romantic attraction—and less conventionally over its legalities. And both Jude and the narrator fall back on gender-essentialist characterizations to explain the thwarting of Jude's aspirations. "Strange difference of sex," muses Jude, as he lies dying, "that time and circumstance, which enlarge the views of most men, narrow the views of women almost invariably" (422). Sue Bridehead and Jude Fawley look toward a future that may never come and that may be terrible if it comes at all, and they pay a high price for their experimentation. Nevertheless, it is possible to discern in *Jude the Obscure* the outlines of a critique of the mutual operation of class and gender boundaries in blighting the aspirations of the male and female subjects they define.

Notes

CHAPTER I

1. Originally Hitchin College, after the town in which it opened in 1869, the college moved to Girton in 1873 (McWilliams-Tullberg, 48, 53). On the history of Girton, see McWilliams-Tullberg; and Stephen.

2. See Davidoff and Hall, 170–71, on Hannah More's use of Saint Paul. See Rendall, *Equal or Different?* 18–19, for a summary of the conventions governing women's public speech.

3. For general discussions of Victorian domestic ideology, see Basch; Burstyn; Ewbank, chap. 1; Poovey, 4–11. On the evangelical roots of domestic ideology, see Davidoff and Hall, chap. 3.

4. For Davies's biography, see Stephen; and Caine, *Victorian Feminists*, chap. 3.

5. Cf. Matthew Arnold's critique, in *Culture and Anarchy,* of "the dealings of Puritanism with the writings of St. Paul" (151), in which he denies that "St. Paul's expression, or any man's expression, can be a perfect and final expression of truth" and advocates approaching Paul's terms "in the fluid way in which St. Paul employs them, and for which alone words are really meant, [and not] in an isolated, fixed, mechanical way, was if they were talismans" (152). Arnold is not, however, concerned with gender.

6. For biographical information about a number of Victorian feminists,

including Butler, see Caine, *Victorian Feminists;* on the range of political and religious beliefs and familial backgrounds of Victorian feminists, see Levine, chap. 2.

7. For histories of the movement see Bryant; and Vicinus, chaps. 4 and 5. On Cambridge specifically, see McWilliams-Tullberg; and Stephen. On Oxford, see Rogers; and Leonardi, chap. 1. Dyhouse is particularly valuable for her coverage of universities other than Oxford and Cambridge. For a skeptical assessment of the achievement of the feminist reformers in the area of girls' education, see Fletcher. For and overview of girls' and womens' education from the Middle Ages on, see Kamm, *Hope Deferred.* Ray Strachey's early (1928), magisterial history of the nineteenth-century women's movement, *The Cause: A Short History of the Women's Movement in Great Britain,* remains a valuable source, particularly chaps. 7, 8, and 13, although much of Strachey's information is covered in later histories.

8. For the debate over the effect on women of their degree status at Cambridge, see McWilliams-Tullberg, 116, 125–27; on the resistance to women's full institutional membership there, see her chaps. 9–11; on the fight for degrees at Oxford, see Rogers; and Leonardi, chap. 1. Inequity remains today for women entering academia. According to Dyhouse, a British report from 1990 "cited figures showing that women still constituted a minority (14 percent) of full-time, tenured university academic staff, and pointed out that this minority was concentrated in lower grade posts" (1).

9. Every historian of Victorian higher education for women discusses the anxiety of the founders and supervisors of the early colleges not to appear to flout convention and decorum—an anxiety that sometimes led to conflict with rebellious students. See Dyhouse, chaps. 2, 3, and 5; Stephen, chap. 14; Vicinus, 145–48.

10. For a seventeenth-century exposition of this position, see Burton.

11. On conduct literature, see Armstrong, chap. 2.

12. For an analysis of the ideological crisis provoked by the governess and other financially embarrassed middle-class women, see Poovey, chap. 5.

13. These women included Frances Mary Buss, founder of the North London Collegiate School, and Dorothea Beale, reforming headmistress of Cheltenham Ladies' School. See Kamm, *How Different from Us.*

14. On the history of the *English Woman's Journal,* see Rendall, "'A Moral Engine.'"

CHAPTER 2

1. For a fuller account of the beginnings of the movement, see chap. 1.

2. On the Brontës' various experiences as teachers and students, see Gérin, 5–16 passim.

3. The sisters' training was hardly competitive, as Gaskell writes: "Of French they knew something; enough to read it fluently, but hardly enough to teach it in competition with natives, or professional masters. Emily and Anne had some

knowledge of music; but here again it was doubtful whether, without more instruction, they could engage to give lessons in it" (Gaskell, 218).

4. On the liminal position of the governess in relation to the class and gender conventions that defined the role of the middle-class woman, see Poovey; and Peterson.

5. In *Shirley* (1849), however, Brontë does depict a downtrodden governess, in the character of Mrs. Pryor; and her epistolary accounts of her own experiences as a governess are unremittingly bitter.

6. As Boumelha remarks, "In the course of the novel, Jane has three jobs, five homes, three families of a sort, two proposals of marriage. If her travel is restricted, at least she nearly goes to the South of France, nearly goes to Madeira, nearly goes to India. She learns French, German and Hindustani. She lives alone, receives male visitors in her bedroom in the middle of the night and hears confidences of financial treachery and sexual profligacy. She saves a life, proposes marriage and gives away thousands of pounds" (75). This mobility contrasts with the more usual pattern of the female *Bildungsroman,* as defined by Abel, Hirsch, and Langland, as opposed to the male *Bildungsroman:* "Women in nineteenth-century fiction are generally unable to leave home for an independent life in the city. When they do, they are not free to explore; more frequently, they merely exchange one domestic sphere for another. While the young hero roams through the city, the young heroine strolls down the country lane. . . . Novels of female development . . . typically substitute inner concentration for active accommodation, rebellion, or withdrawal" (8).

7. *Jane Eyre* has been read as a novel of female self-education throughout its history. Lewes asserted in 1847 that "It *is* an autobiography,—not, perhaps, in the naked facts and circumstances, but in the actual suffering and experience" (691). Gilbert and Gubar call *Jane Eyre* "a distinctively female *Bildungsroman* in which the problems encountered by the protagonist . . . are symptomatic of difficulties Everywoman in a patriarchal society must meet and overcome" (339). Bodenheimer suggests that "Jane Eyre's history may be read as the story of an empowered narrator, which describes her gradual, though partial release from conventional bondages, both social and fictional" (98).

8. For another discussion of Jane's relationship to her imagination, see Homans, *Bearing the Word,* chap. 4.

9. Brontë chillingly summed up, in a letter to her brother, the opinion of her fellow teachers at the Pensionnat Heger on which Lucy's clearly draws: "They have not intellect or politeness or good-nature or good feeling. They are nothing" (qtd. in Gérin, 230).

10. Rigby, in her hostile review of *Jane Eyre,* mocks this isolation as implausible: "Jane had lived [at Lowood] for eight years with 110 girls and fifteen teachers. Why had she formed no friendships among them? . . . Of course it suited the author's end to represent the heroine as utterly destitute of the common means of

assistance, in order to exhibit both her trials and her powers of self-support—the whole book rests on this assumption—but it is one which, under the circumstances, is very unnatural and very unjust" (173). It is, however, Rigby herself who declares that the governess "has no equals, and therefore can have no sympathy. . . . She must, to all intents and purposes, live alone" (177). Eagleton argues that "[Brontë's] fiction portrays the unprotected self in its lonely conquest of harsh conditions, and so intimates a meritocratic vision; but individualist self-reliance leads you to roles and relations which are objectively fitting," (*Myths of Power,* 26).

11. Female homosocial community is represented as even more sinister in *Villette,* in which Lucy experiences Madame Beck's school as a paradoxical nightmare of omnipresent surveillance and total isolation—until she develops a friendship with M. Paul Emmanuel.

12. On Brontë's ambivalent representation of female communities in *Jane Eyre* and *Villette,* see Nestor, chap. 5.

13. For erotic energy within women's intellectual communities as both a bonding and an unsettling force, see Vicinus, *Independent Women,* 157–62; 187–210.

14. On the equality between Jane and Rochester, see also Gilbert and Gubar, 352–54.

15. For Barbara Hardy, for example, Jane's decision to leave Rochester confirms a "weakness of the [novel's] moral pattern" that comes from "imposing an ideology on to a realistic psychological pattern" (27).

16. The quotations are from, respectively, Moglen, 130; Rich, 102; and Showalter, *A Literature of Their Own,* 124. For recent interpretations that question Jane's achievement of individualistic subjectivity, see London; and Marcus.

17. In fact, Brontë's first novel—*The Professor*—has a male first-person narrator. It is also notable that *Shirley,* which has a third-person, omniscient narrator, also contains the greatest amount of explicit discussion of gender roles; Caroline Helstone is the most thoroughly marked as "feminine" of any of Brontë's female protagonists, and Shirley's transgression of gender boundaries is thematized.

18. For a different reading of this similarity, see Poovey, 146–47.

19. London makes a related argument for a reading of *Jane Eyre* as a narrative that produces a disciplined and submissive, not an expressive and self-authorizing, subject. Although she does not discuss Adele, she points to the ways that Jane, in depicting her past acts, restages "the disciplinary scenes of childhood . . . in the theater of the adult self" and "comes increasingly to represent not only the child being beaten but the punishing agency" (201).

20. For a different interpretation of this point, cf. Poovey: "Even though Jane marries Rochester, then, she does so as an expression of her desire, not as the self-sacrifice St. John advocates; the image with which she represents her marriage fuses man and woman instead of respecting their separate bodies, much less their separate spheres. 'Ever more absolutely bone of his bone and flesh of his flesh,' Jane represents herself as taking the law of coverture to its logical extreme" (147). For

Poovey, this fusion represents a subversion of gender essentialism, rather than a slide into solipsism. For other discussions of the ending as representing a diminishment of desire and/or a turn away from the social, see Gilbert and Gubar, 369–70; and Ohmann, 763.

21. On the correspondences in social significance between men of letters and women, see David, 10–14.

CHAPTER 3

1. There is also an animated version of *The King and I* from Warner Brothers (1999).

2. *The Romance of the Harem* was retitled *Siamese Harem Life* for a 1952 reprint; as Morgan observes, "The effect of the change is clearly to lay claim to being historical description rather than historical inventions" (*Romance of the Harem*, xxv).

3. In the discussion that follows, for consistency with Leonowens's own nineteenth-century usage, I refer to the country now known as Thailand as "Siam." Associated with a history of absolute monarchy, the name "Siam" was changed to "Thailand" by the premier Pibul Songgram in 1938, following the institution of constitutional monarchy.

4. *The English Governess* also marks its factual basis by including nonnarrative materials, such as a facsimile reproduction of a letter from King Chulalongkorn acknowledging receipt of a sympathy letter on the death of his father.

5. In addition to publishing four books, Leonowens traveled to Russia in 1880 to write a series of articles for the Boston-based magazine *Youth's Companion;* founded an art college in Halifax, Canada; campaigned for women's suffrage and other causes; and supervised the education of eight grandchildren (see Dow, 75, 93–96).

6. Zlotnick reads *Jane Eyre* and *The English Governess* together as texts of "maternal imperialism," finding that where Jane's narrative, with the aid of the Victorian marriage plot, successfully negotiates its heroine's liberation within the bounds of domestic ideology, Leonowens's narrative fails to do so: "Leonowens's identity constantly threatens to melt into that of her dark double in a way Jane's never does because female influence, the power afforded women by the ideology of domesticity, cannot easily be sustained outside the domestic worlds of Victorian fiction" (48). With the outlines of this argument I substantially agree, although my own emphasizes that the "domestic worlds of Victorian fiction" have more than one "outside"—in this case, the story of successful upward mobility that Leonowens chooses not to tell, as well as the more ambiguous story that she does.

7. In addition to Kaplan, recent analyses of the Leonowens narratives and their revisions include Brown; Donaldson; and Morgan, *Place Matters*.

8. See Mills's summary of "Othering" conventions in travel writing (87–91); and Said's summary of Orientalist assumptions (206 and passim*)*.

9. Leonowens's one mention of herself in *Our Asiatic Cousins* is in the third person: "For nearly seven years did the English governess at the Court of Siam devote her life, health, and best efforts to the education, moral and spiritual elevation of her large class of royal pupils, fostering with jealous care every high quality, every noble impulse and every lofty aspiration in them all; but above all in the heir-apparent, who was one day to become the sole arbiter of the future destiny of millions of our Asiatic cousins" (360).

10. For the importance of Siam within the colonial ambitions of the British and French, as well as the Americans, and Mongkut's successful diplomacy in resisting those ambitions, see Chakrabongse, chap. 4; and Moffatt, chaps. 4–6.

11. Mills argues that Said's characterization of Orientalism to some degree helps to construct the very exclusion it claims to discover: "Despite Said's useful critique, he risks becoming entangled himself in this very male view of imperialism since he ignores the fact that many women were actively involved in colonialism: they wrote about the colonial situation and their works were very widely read" (58). Although it is true that women travel writers were "widely read," the predominant reception of female-authored texts, as Mills herself argues (chap. 4), evaluated them as less authoritative or constitutive of "knowledge" than men's; that is, they were not part of the Orientalist establishment.

12. On the nineteenth-century reception of Leonowens's texts, see Morgan, *Place Matters,* 246–48.

13. See, for example, Chakrabongse, 209–11; Griswold, 44–49; and Moffatt, app. 4. The Thai government apparently discouraged distribution of Leonowens's texts (Landon, 357); both *The King and I* (1956) and *Anna and the King* (1999) have been banned in Thailand (http://www.thaistudents.com/kingandi/index.html), where all versions of the story continue to be resented as gross distortions of Thai history and acts of *lèse-majesté.* A list of *Anna and the King*'s offenses released by the Thai government includes "[a]ttempting to suggest to the innocent that the teaching of Anna Leonowens was a factor that enabled His Majesty King Chulalongkorn to preserve the independence of his country, abolish slavery and introduce religious freedom and reform the justice system. . . . It is suspected that the inclusion of such suggestion is motivated by the jealously [*sic*] of certain western races that could not tolerate the success of an oriental nation which managed to preserve its independence and introducing [*sic*] far reaching reforms. Thus, it must attribute part of such success to Anna Leonowens whom they thought belonged to the superior race but who was in fact an individual with doubtful origin and could even be half Indian" (http://www.thaistudents.com/kingandi/reasons.html; 3.6). Notably, even this voice of state authority that indicts Orientalist prejudice turns to Leonowens's "doubtful origin[s]," and particularly her doubtful national and racial origins, to discredit her.

14. On this point, cf. Morgan, introduction to *The Romance of the Harem,* xi.

15. For an overview of Josephine Butler's life and work, see Caine, *Victorian Feminists,* chap. 5; for her work in India, see Burton, chap. 5; on Mary Carpenter, see Burton, 109–13, 122–23.

16. See Dow, 67–69, for the composition of *The English Governess* and *Romance of the Harem;* both began life as articles in the American *Atlantic Monthly.* According to Griswold, Leonowens later admitted that "readers wanted sensational revelations about the Orient and she had to provide them in order to satisfy her publisher" (49; Griswold gives no source for this claim. Cf. Dow, 123). Brown points out that Leonowens wrote "primarily for a postwar U.S. audience" (603), not an English one, an audience that, Brown argues, provides a context for Leonowens's adoption of "U.S. feminist abolitionist imagery and discourse" (604). Perhaps it also, by virtue of being yet another location that is not-England, enables the consolidation of Leonowens's claim to national and class status—to being an English woman.

17. For an analysis of such a triumph of feminine values in an eighteenth-century novel, Samuel Richardson's *Pamela,* see Armstrong, 108–34.

18. In their second meeting as employer and employee, Rochester declares to Jane, "'It would please me now to draw you out—: to learn more of you—therefore speak.' Instead of speaking, I smiled; and not a very complacent or submissive smile either. . . . 'If he expects me to talk for the mere sake of talking and showing off, he will find he has addressed himself to the wrong person,' I thought" (139).

19. More than fifty years earlier, the less temperate Mary Wollstonecraft drew the analogy more plainly: "In a seraglio, I grant, that all these arts (of feigned delicacy) are necessary; the epicure must have his palate tickled, or he will sink into apathy; but have women so little ambition as to be satisfied with such a condition? Can they supinely [*sic*] dream life away in the lap of pleasure, or the languor of weariness, rather than assert their claim to pursue reasonable pleasures, and render themselves conspicuous by practicing the virtues which dignify mankind?" (112).

20. Although he functions in *The English Governess* to remind the reader of Leonowens's position as both widow and mother, the historical Louis Leonowens will prove an ungovernable child (see Bristowe; also Dow, 67–70) and will run away from school to Siam to make his fortune in the teak industry. Leonowens's maternal self-representation is in any case intermittent and unconvincing.

21. On representations of Victoria as a wife and mother, see Homans, *Royal Representations,* 17–32.

22. Birkett, in her account of Victorian women travelers, identifies such usages as common: May French-Sheldon in East Africa is addressed as "Sabe" (sir), Mary Gaunt in Peking as "gentleman," and Gertrude Bell as "effendi, a Turkish title of respect given to professional men" (117).

23. In addition to Ahmed, see Grewal; Kroller; Melman; Morgan, "Victorian Women, Wisdom, and Southeast Asia," 216–24; and Zonana.

24. This representation of women of the harem as indolent is conventional. Compare, for example, Martineau's 1848 account of her visit to a harem in *Eastern Life, Present and Past:* "The poor ladies cannot conceive of one's having anything to do. . . . To sit hour after hour on the deewán [divan], without any exchange of ideas, having our clothes examined, and being plied with successive cups of coffee and sherbet, and pipes, and being gazed at by a half-circle of girls in brocade and shawls, and made to sit down again as soon as one attempts to rise, is as wearisome an experience as one meets with in foreign lands" (239).

25. See Morgan, *Place Matters,* 256–63, for an argument that *The Romance of the Harem* offers "frequent testimonials to the rhetorical eloquence, the powerful voices, of the women in Siam." Morgan argues that Leonowens's frequent dialogue and first-person narrative, as well as her representation of herself as "the mimetic recorder or literal transcriber rather than the overseeing interpreter" (258–59), mitigates the "generally imperializing quality of the rhetorical structure of *The Romance*" (258). My own argument places more stress on the frequently nonnaturalistic and highly rhetorical speech that Leonowens attributes to her narrators, making it difficult to read them as mimetic recordings or transcriptions.

26. As Kaplan puts it, "Part memsahib, part feminist avenger and adventurer, the fictionalizations of Leonowens speak to the desire for a good mother or a powerful woman who can stand up to patriarchal authority" (48).

CHAPTER 4

1. Eliot began work on the story of Lydgate and the Vincys, a narrative called "Middlemarch," in 1869; she did not begin "Miss Brooke," then a separate story, until 1870. For an account of the novel's composition and development, see Carroll's introduction to *Middlemarch.*

2. On *Middlemarch* as "critical of [Eliot's] own and her age's faith in knowledge," see Welsh, 136. On *Middlemarch* and women's education, see Beer, 172–79. On Eliot as an intellectual, see Cottom, particularly chaps. 1 and 2; and David, chap. 9.

3. Beer suggests: "The first reviewers of *Middlemarch* were in little doubt about the book's intended topic: it was the nature and the education of women, and the question of society's responsibility for women's difficulties" (147). Some contemporary reviewers, however, protested that attempts—including Eliot's in the prelude and conclusion—to fit *Middlemarch* into the frame of the "Woman Question" were misleading. See, for example, R. H. Hutton, Sidney Colvin, A. V. Dicey, and H. Lawrenny, all in Carroll.

4. David, for example, attributes her hesitancy to her own investment, as a self-made female "sage," in the status quo (177–80); Austen summarizes critiques of Eliot's antifeminism while defending her position; Showalter, "Greening of Sister George," also comes to Eliot's defense.

5. David, who characterizes this letter as Davies's "describ[ing] her increasing

frustration when confronted by Eliot's evasion of political action through a kind of meandering discourse" (177) is in no doubt of Davies's impatience and sarcasm here; her reading is persuasive, although I think it is less a matter of fact than interpretation. Davies seems early to have been aware of the possibility of hesitancy on Eliot's part, writing to Bodichon in 1868, "It is rather curious that [Eliot] should be the only person who favors [the college] to you. I should not have wondered much if she had been against" (qtd. in Stephen, 169).

6. In the same early letter in which she reproaches Davies for her "hurrying industrial view of life," for example, she insists: "We can not afford to part with that exquisite type of gentleness, tenderness, possible maternity suffusing a woman's being with affectionateness, which makes what we mean by the feminine character" (qtd. in Stephen, 182).

7. For a related analysis of Eliot's use of the metaphor of "moral currency," which also concerns the degradation of cultural forms, see Gallagher, *Industrial Reformation,* 252–63.

8. Maggie's own education, which substitutes imaginative and religious literature for Euclid and Latin, is no better preparation for their changed circumstances. As Tom has been ill served in his new need for practical skills, Maggie has been ill served in her new need for spiritual comfort, a need finally met by Bob Jakin's unwitting gift of Thomas à Kempis. But Maggie's education at least does not dull her sensibilities the way Tom's does his.

9. Jacobus finds Eliot in *Mill on the Floss* using metaphor, "improper, [and] disrespectful of authorities" (73), to undermine the authority of "maxims" and to reinvigorate the fossilizations of patriarchal language. Similarly, the problem that Eliot identifies here with metaphors about women is not the use of a particular form of literary language, nor the feminine qualities celebrated by the metaphor, but the availability of those metaphors to commodification within middle-class culture.

10. Graver points out the specific parallels between Mill's discussion of marriage in "On the Subjection of Women" and Eliot's description of the Rosamond/Lydgate marriage; she also points to Lydgate's complicity in the "system" that destroys him (205–9).

11. "It is almost impossible," wrote Elizabeth Wolstenholme in 1869, "to convey to any one who has had no experience in teaching girls any notion of the wholly unsystematic and confused state of their education" (294–95).

12. Armstrong finds such "hypergamy," or marriage up, positively represented at the novel's commencement in *Pamela* (131). If, as Armstrong suggests, the power of hypergamy is a positive one in Richardson's novel, bearing the capacity for middle-class reform of aristocratic privilege, it has become far more suspect by the time that Eliot is writing, representing instead the possible commodification of the values of the domestic ideal.

13. Ladislaw's intellectual cosmopolitanism seems to be similar to that which,

as Gallagher demonstrates, Eliot particularly deplores in "The Modern Hep! Hep! Hep!" in *Theophrastus Such* (Gallagher, "George Eliot and *Daniel Deronda*," 39–62). In *Middlemarch*, the love of a good woman and his association with her family appear to recall Will from his alienated wanderings to put his knowledge into the service of the English state; but Will's state of mind about vocation is so much less clearly rendered than Lydgate's and Dorothea's that the transition from dilettantism to service remains vague.

14. Cf. Kucich: "Ultimately, George Eliot is unable to imagine what interdependence would be like as the fulfillment of a desire. . . . There is a countermovement of desire within Eliot's central characters that can be seen to divert them from any orientation to others at all, and to turn them irrevocably inward instead" (117).

15. Books are the similarly independent Maggie Tulliver's escape from the unbearably constricting demands of her family and situation, especially when they come to be associated with her illicit meetings with Philip: "It has been very sweet, I know—" she tells him, "all the talking together, and the books, and the feeling that I had the walk to look forward to when I could tell you the thoughts that had come into my head while I was away from you. But it has made me restless—it has made me think a great deal about the world; and I have impatient thoughts again—I get weary of my home" (*Mill on the Floss*, 436).

16. On fictional representations of women readers, see Flint, chap. 9.

17. David suggests that Eliot's female characters particularly bear the weight of her nostalgic vision: "It is female characters who often become metaphors for nostalgic conservatism, emblems of Eliot's residual desire (as a traditional intellectual) to affiliate herself with the land-owning classes in England rather than with the liberal, educated middle classes which encouraged and eventually adored her" (167).

18. That Eliot's fiction evades the social and historical questions it raises, by turning either from the present to the past or from the social to the personal, is a frequent burden of Eliot criticism. On *Middlemarch* in particular, see Cottom, 158–59; Eagleton, "George Eliot: Ideology and Literary Form," 38–40; and Kucich, chap. 2, 131–51, and passim. Recently, Staten has argued, to the contrary, for *Middlemarch* as an exemplary historical novel, on the grounds that "[o]ne would have to be strangely submissive to the authority of narratorial telling to hear [Eliot's] moralizing as the novel's last word. For what the novel *shows* is history woven into the text in a scrupulous and critical fashion that overflows the narrator's moralism" (992).

CHAPTER 5

1. For an overview of nineteenth-century sociobiological theories of sexual differentiation as they bear upon the construction of femininity, see Russett. For a more detailed account than I can give here of "the growing medicalisation of sexuality" during the latter half of the nineteenth century, see Boumelha, 11–25. For further examples of gynecological antifeminism, see Showalter, *Female Malady*.

For another discussion of *Jude the Obscure* and late-Victorian constructions of femininity, see Brady.

2. For the conflicts over Hardy's interment and the literary executorship, see Millgate, 574–77; and Gittings, 211–13. Millgate writes that "[o]nce Hardy was dead Cockerell and Barrie began to assert their male authority over what Cockerell (in a letter to his wife) had already referred to as 'the housefull of women'" (574). Gittings emphasizes particularly the contrast between "[Hardy's] humble beginning [and] his exalted ending" (211).

3. For a summary of the tensions in the construction of the literary profession, particularly in the nineteenth century, see Poovey, 101–8.

4. Poovey's definition of "literary discourse" does not distinguish significantly between fiction and nonfiction prose. By contrast, Christ, in her analysis of Carlyle's "The Hero as Man of Letters," argues that "In Carlyle's construction . . . the novel['s] . . . feminization provides the only exception to his heroic masculinization of the world of letters" (20). I am suggesting, like Poovey, that the field of literature *in general* was structurally feminized (hence the need for heroic masculinization); I am distinguishing the novel, however, as particularly subject to feminization for the reasons discussed in this section.

5. On the marriage of Jane Welsh and Thomas Carlyle, see Rose, 25–44, 243–59.

6. For an interesting discussion of Jude and Sue as inhabiting "a word of verbal echoes," see Weinstein 125–45.

7. Phillotson says of Sue that "her intellect sparkles like diamonds, while mine smoulders like brown paper" (241); the narrator describes her as having "an intellect [that] scintillated like a star" (361), and Jude calls her "a woman-poet, a woman-seer, a woman whose soul shone like a diamond—whom all the wise of the world would have been proud of" (369) and "a woman whose intellect was to mine like a star to a benzoline lamp" (422).

8. On this point, see Langland, who argues that "Sue both is and is not a typical woman, depending on Jude's psychosocial investment in her. At those points when he fears he will lose her, he tends to brand her typical of her sex to distance himself from his need for her" (39).

Works Cited

PRIMARY SOURCES

Arnold, Matthew. *Culture and Anarchy.* Edited by J. Dover Wilson. Cambridge: Cambridge University Press, 1960.

Barrett Browning, Elizabeth. *Aurora Leigh: A Poem.* Introduction by Gardner B. Taplin. Chicago: Academy Chicago, 1979.

Brontë, Charlotte. *Jane Eyre.* Edited by Margaret Smith. New York: Oxford University Press, 1993.

———. *Villette.* Edited by Margaret Smith and Herbert Rosengarten. New York: Oxford University Press, 1984.

———. *Shirley.* Edited by Herbert Rosengarten and Margaret Smith. New York: Oxford University Press, 1979.

Burton, J[ohn]. *Lectures on Female Education and Manners.* London, 1793.

Butler, Josephine. "The Education and Employment of Women." 1868. In *The Education Papers: Women's Quest for Equality in Britain, 1850–1912,* edited by Dale Spender. Women's Source Library. New York: Routledge and Kegan Paul, 1987.

Carroll, David, ed. *George Eliot: The Critical Heritage.* London: Routledge and Kegan Paul, 1971.

Davies, Emily. *The Higher Education of Women (1866).* Edited by Janet Haworth. London: Hambledon Press, 1988.

———. "Family Chronicle." In *The Papers of Emily Davies and Barbara Bodichon, from Girton College, Cambridge.* Microform. 14 reels. Brighton, Sussex: Harvester Microforms, 1985.

———. "Home and the Higher Education." In *The Education Papers: Women's Quest for Equality in Britain, 1850–1912,* edited by Dale Spender. Women's Source Library. New York: Routledge and Kegan Paul, 1987.

Eliot, George. *The George Eliot Letters.* Edited by Gordon Haight. 9 vols. New Haven: Yale University Press, 1955–78.

———. *Middlemarch.* Edited by David Carroll. New York: Oxford University Press, 1988.

———. *The Mill on the Floss.* Edited by A. S. Byatt. New York: Viking Penguin, 1979.

———. *Selected Essays, Poems, and Other Writings.* Edited by A. S. Byatt and Nicholas Warren. New York: Penguin, 1990.

Ellis, Sarah Stickney. *The Women of England: Their Social Duties, and Domestic Habits.* Vol. 1. Philadelphia, 1839.

"Female Education." *Quarterly Review* 126 (April 1869): 448–79.

Hardy, Thomas. *Jude the Obscure.* Edited by Patricia Ingham. New York: Oxford University Press, 1985.

———. *The Life and Works of Thomas Hardy.* Edited by Michael Millgate. Athens: University of Georgia Press, 1985.

———. *A Pair of Blue Eyes.* Edited by Alan Manford. Oxford: Oxford University Press, 1985.

———. *The Return of the Native.* Edited by Tony Slade. New York: Penguin, 1999.

———. *Tess of the D'Urbervilles.* Edited by Juliet Grindle and Simon Gatrell. New York: Oxford University Press, 1983.

———. *The Woodlanders.* New York: Viking Penguin, 1981.

Landon, Margaret. *Anna and the King of Siam.* New York: John Day Co., 1944.

Leonowens, Anna. *The English Governess at the Siamese Court.* 1870. New York: Oxford University Press, 1988.

———. *The Romance of the Harem.* 1873. Edited by Susan Morgan. Charlottesville: University of Virginia Press, 1991.

Lerner, Lawrence, and John Holmstrom, eds. *Thomas Hardy and His Readers: A Selection of Contemporary Reviews.* London: The Bodley Head, 1968.

[Lewes, G. H.]. "Recent Novels: French and English." *Fraser's Magazine* 36 (December 1847).

Martineau, Harriet. *Eastern Life, Present and Past.* Philadelphia, 1848.

Maudsley, Henry. "Sex in Mind and Education." *Fortnightly Review,* n.s. 21 (1874): 466–83.

Maynard, Constance L. Autobiography. *The Diaries of Constance Maynard* (microform holograph). Reels 13–14. *The Origins of Modern Feminism, Part I.* Brighton, Sussex: Harvester Microform, 1987. 14 Reels. Originals at Queen Mary College, University of London.

Mill, John Stuart. *On Liberty.* Edited by David Spitz. New York: Norton, 1975.

———. "On the Subjection of Women." In *Essays on Sex Equality,* by John Stuart

Mill and Harriet Taylor Mill. Edited by Alice S. Rossi. Chicago: University of Chicago Press, 1970.

[Parkes, Bessie Rayner]. "The Profession of the Teacher: The Annual Reports of the GBI from 1843 to 1856." *English Woman's Journal* 1, no. 4 (June 1858).

Phillips, Ann, ed. *A Newnham Anthology*. Cambridge: Cambridge University Press, 1979.

Review of *Intellectual Education, and Its Influence on the Character and Happiness of Women* by Emily Shirreff. *English Woman's Journal* 1, no. 5 (July 1858).

Ricks, Christopher, ed. *The Poems of Tennyson*. New York: W. W. Norton, 1972.

Rigby, Elizabeth (Lady Eastlake). "Vanity Fair—and Jane Eyre." *Quarterly Review* 84 (1848): 153–85.

Ruskin, John. "Of Queen's Gardens." 1864. In *The Complete Works of John Ruskin,* edited by E. T. Cook and Alexander Wedderburn. The Library Edition. Vol. 13: 109–44. London: George Allen; New York: Longman's, Green and Co., 1905.

Shirreff, Emily. *Intellectual Education, and Its Influence on the Character and Happiness of Women.* London, 1858.

Spender, Dale, ed. *The Education Papers: Women's Quest for Equality in Britain, 1850–1912.* Women's Source Library. New York: Routledge and Kegan Paul, 1987.

Wollstonecraft, Mary. A *Vindication of the Rights of Woman.* 1792. Edited by Miram Brody. Reprint, New York: Penguin, 1985.

Wolstenholme-Elmy, Elizabeth. 1869. "The Education of Girls." In *The Education Papers: Women's Quest for Equality in Britain 1850–1912,* edited by Dale Spender. Women's Source Library. New York: Routledge and Kegan Paul, 1987.

SECONDARY SOURCES

Abel, Elizabeth, Marianne Hirsch, and Elizabeth Langland, eds. *The Voyage In: Fictions of Female Development*. Hanover, N.H.: University Press of New England, 1983.

Ahmed, Leila. "Western Ethnocentrism and Perceptions of the Harem." *Feminist Studies* 8 (fall 1982): 521–34.

Armstrong, Nancy. *Desire and Domestic Fiction: A Political History of the Novel.* Oxford: Oxford University Press, 1987.

Austen, Zelda. "Why Feminist Critics Are Angry with George Eliot." *College English* 37 (February 1976): 549–61.

Basch, Francoise. *Relative Creatures: Victorian Women in Society and the Novel.* New York: Schocken Books, 1974.

Beer, Gillian. *George Eliot.* Bloomington: Indiana University Press, 1986.

Birkett, Dea. *Spinsters Abroad: Victorian Lady Explorers.* New York: Oxford, 1989.

Bloom, Harold, ed. *Charlotte Brontë's "Jane Eyre."* New York: Chelsea House, 1987.

Bodenheimer, Rosemarie. "Jane Eyre in Search of Her Story." *Papers on Language and Literature* 16 (fall 1980): 387–402. Reprinted in *Charlotte Brontë's "Jane Eyre,"* edited by Harold Bloom. New York: Chelsea House, 1987.

Boumelha, Penny. *Thomas Hardy and Women: Sexual Ideology and Narrative Form.* Sussex: Harvester Press, 1982.

————. *Charlotte Brontë.* New York: Harvester Wheatsheaf, 1990.

Bradbrook, M. C. *"That Infidel Place": A Short History of Girton College, 1869–1969.* London: Chatto and Windus, 1969.

Brady, Kristin. "Textual Hysteria: Hardy's Narrator on Women." In *The Sense of Sex: Feminist Perspectives on Hardy,* edited by Margaret Higonnet, pp. 87–131. Urbana and Chicago: University of Illinois Press, 1993.

Bristowe, W. S. *Louis and the King of Siam.* New York: Thai-American Publishers, 1976.

Brown, Susan. "Alternatives to the Missionary Position: Anna Leonowens as Victorian Travel Writer." *Feminist Studies* 21 (fall 1995): 587–614.

Bryant, Margaret. *The Unexpected Revolution: A Study in the History of the Education of Girls and Women in the Nineteenth Century.* London: University of London, Institute of Education, 1979.

Burstyn, Joan N. *Victorian Education and the Ideal of Womanhood.* Totowa, N.J.: Barnes and Noble, 1980.

Burton, Antoinette. *Burdens of History: British Feminists, Indian Women, and Imperial Culture, 1865–1915.* Chapel Hill: University of North Carolina Press, 1994.

Caine, Barbara. *Victorian Feminists.* New York: Oxford University Press, 1992.

Carroll, David. Introduction to *Middlemarch,* by George Eliot. New York: Oxford University Press, 1988.

Chakrabongse, Chula. *Lords of Life: The Paternal Monarchy of Bangkok, 1782–1932.* London: Alvin Redman, 1960.

Christ, Carol. "'The Hero as Man of Letters': Masculinity and Victorian Nonfiction Prose." In *Victorian Sages and Cultural Discourse: Renegotiating Gender and Power,* edited by Thaïs E. Morgan. New Brunswick, N.J.: Rutgers University Press, 1990.

Cottom, Daniel. *Social Figures: George Eliot, Social History, and Literary Representation.* Minneapolis: University of Minnesota Press, 1987.

Dale, Peter A. "Thomas Hardy and the Best Consummation Possible." In *Nature Transfigured: Science and Literature, 1700–1900,* edited by John Christie and Sally Shuttleworth. Manchester: Manchester University Press, 1989.

David, Deirdre. *Intellectual Women and Victorian Patriarchy: Harriet Martineau, Elizabeth Barrett Browning, George Eliot.* Ithaca, N.Y.: Cornell University Press, 1987.

Davidoff, Lenore, and Catherine Hall. *Family Fortunes: Men and Women of the English Middle Class, 1780–1850.* London: Hutchinson, 1987.

Donaldson, Laura. *"The King and I* in *Uncle Tom's Cabin,* or On the Border of the Women's Room." *Cinema Journal* 29 (spring 1990): 53–68.

Dow, Leslie Smith. *Anna Leonowens: A Life Beyond the King and I.* Nova Scotia: Pottersfield Press, 1991.

Dowling, Linda. *Hellenism and Homosexuality in Victorian Oxford*. Ithaca: Cornell University Press, 1994.

Dyhouse, Carol. *No Distinction of Sex? Women in British Universities, 1870–1939*. London: UCL Press, 1995.

Eagleton, Terry. "George Eliot: Ideology and Literary Form." In *Criticism and Ideology: A Study in Marxist Literary Theory*, edited by Terry Eagleton. London: Verso, 1976. Reprinted in Middlemarch, *George Eliot*, edited by John Peck. New York: St. Martin's, 1992. 33–44.

———. *Myths of Power: A Marxist Study of the Brontës*. 2d ed. London: Macmillan, 1988.

Ewbank, Inga Stina. *Their Proper Sphere: A Study of the Brontë Sisters as Early Victorian Novelists*. London: Edward Arnold, 1966.

Fletcher, Sheila. *Feminists and Bureaucrats*. New York: Cambridge University Press, 1980.

Flint, Kate. *The Woman Reader, 1837–1914*. Oxford: Clarendon Press, 1993.

Gallagher, Catherine. *The Industrial Reformation of English Fiction: Social Discourse and Narrative Form, 1832–1867*. Chicago: University of Chicago Press, 1985.

———. "George Eliot and *Daniel Deronda:* The Prostitute and the Jewish Question." In *Sex, Politics, and Science in the Nineteenth-Century Novel*, edited by Ruth Bernard Yeazell. Baltimore: Johns Hopkins University Press, 1986.

Gaskell, Elizabeth. *The Life of Charlotte Brontë*. Edited by Alan Shelston. New York: Penguin, 1975.

Gérin, Winifred. *Charlotte Brontë: The Evolution of Genius*. London: Oxford University Press, 1967.

Gilbert, Sandra M., and Susan Gubar. *The Madwoman in the Attic: The Woman Writer and the Nineteenth-Century Literary Imagination*. New Haven: Yale University Press, 1979.

Gittings, Robert. *Thomas Hardy's Later Years*. Boston: Little, Brown, 1978.

Glendinning, Victoria. *A Suppressed Cry: Life and Death of a Quaker Daughter*. London: Routledge and Kegan Paul, 1969.

Graver, Suzanne. *George Eliot and Community: A Study in Social Theory and Fictional Form*. Berkeley: University of California Press, 1984.

Grewal, Inderpal. *Home and Harem: Nation, Gender, Empire, and the Cultures of Travel*. Durham, N.C.: Duke University Press, 1996.

Griswold, A. B. *King Mongkut of Siam*. New York: Asia Society, 1961.

Hardy, Barbara. "Providence Invoked: Dogmatic Form in *Jane Eyre* and *Robinson Crusoe*." In *The Appropriate Form: An Essay on the Novel*. Reprinted in *Charlotte Brontë's "Jane Eyre,"* edited by Harold Bloom. New York: Chelsea House, 1987.

Hardy, Evelyn, and F. B. Pinion, eds. *One Rare Fair Woman: Thomas Hardy's Letters to Florence Henniker, 1893–1922*. London: Macmillan, 1972.

Helsinger, Elizabeth K., Robin Lauterbach Sheets, and William Veeder. *The Woman Question: Society and Literature in England and America, 1837–1883*. 3 vols. Chicago: University of Chicago Press, 1989.

Higonnet, Margaret, ed. *The Sense of Sex: Feminist Perspectives on Hardy*. Urbana and Chicago: University of Illinois Press, 1993.

Homans, Margaret. *Bearing the Word: Language and Female Experience in Nineteenth-Century Women's Writing*. Chicago: University of Chicago Press, 1986.

———. *Royal Representations: Queen Victoria and British Culture, 1837–1876*. Chicago: University of Chicago Press, 1998.

Howarth, Janet. Introduction to *The Higher Education of Women (1866)*, by Emily Davies. London: Hambledon Press, 1988.

Jacobus, Mary. "Men of Maxims and *The Mill on the Floss*." In *Reading Woman: Essays in Feminist Criticism,* edited by Mary Jacobus. New York: Columbia University Press, 1986.

Kamm, Josephine. *Hope Deferred: Girls' Education in English History*. London: Methuen, 1965.

———. *How Different from Us: A Biography of Miss Buss and Miss Beale*. London: Bodley Head, 1958.

Kaplan, Caren. "'Getting to Know You': Travel, Gender, and the Politics of Representation in *Anna and the King of Siam* and *The King and I*." In *Late Imperial Culture*, edited by Román De La Campa, E. Ann Kaplan, and Michael Sprinker, pp. 33–52. London: Verso, 1995.

Kroller, Eva-Marie. "First Impressions: Rhetorical Strategies in Travel Writing by Victorian Women." *ARIEL: A Review of International English Literature* 21, no. 4 (October 1990): 87–99.

Kucich, John. *Repression in Victorian Fiction: Charlotte Brontë, George Eliot, and Charles Dickens*. Berkeley: University of California Press, 1987.

Langland, Elizabeth. "Becoming a Man in *Jude the Obscure*." In *The Sense of Sex: Feminist Perspectives on Hardy,* edited by Margaret Higonnet. Urbana and Chicago: University of Illinois Press, 1993.

Leonardi, Susan. *Dangerous by Degrees: Women at Oxford and the Somerville College Novelists*. New Brunswick, N.J.: Rutgers University Press, 1989.

Levine, Philippa. *Feminist Lives in Victorian England: Private Roles and Public Commitment*. Oxford and Cambridge: Blackwell, 1990.

London, Bette. "The Pleasures of Submission: *Jane Eyre* and the Production of the Text." *ELH* 58 (1991): 195–213.

McWilliams-Tullberg, Rita. *Women at Cambridge*. Rev. ed. Cambridge: Cambridge University Press, 1998.

Marcus, Sharon. "The Profession of the Author: Abstraction, Advertising, and *Jane Eyre*." *PMLA* 110, no. 2 (March 1995): 206–19.

Melman, Billie. *Women's Orients: English Women and the Middle East, 1718–1918*. Ann Arbor: University of Michigan Press, 1992.

Michie, Helena. *Sororophobia*. New York: Oxford University Press, 1992.

Millgate, Michael. *Thomas Hardy: A Biography*. Oxford: Oxford University Press, 1982.

Mills, Sara. *Discourses of Difference: An Analysis of Women's Travel Writing and Colonialism*. New York: Routledge, 1991.

Moffat, Abbot Low. *Mongkut, the King of Siam*. Ithaca, N.Y.: Cornell University Press, 1961.

Moglen, Helene. *Charlotte Brontë: The Self Conceived*. New York: Norton, 1976.

Morgan, Susan. *Place Matters: Gendered Geography in Victorian Women's Travel Books about Southeast Asia*. New Brunswick, N.J.: Rutgers University Press, 1996.

———. "Victorian Women, Wisdom, and Southeast Asia." In *Victorian Sages and Cultural Discourse: Renegotiating Gender and Power*, edited by Thaïs E. Morgan. New Brunswick, N.J.: Rutgers University Press, 1990.

Nestor, Pauline. *Female Friendships and Communities: Charlotte Brontë, George Eliot, Elizabeth Gaskell*. New York: Oxford University Press, 1985.

Ohmann, Carol. "Historical Reality and 'Divine Appointment' in Charlotte Brontë's Fiction." *Signs* 2, no. 4 (summer 1977): 757–78.

Peterson, M. Jeanne. "The Victorian Governess: Status Incongruence in Family and Society." In *Suffer and Be Still: Women and the Victorian Age*, edited by Martha Vicinus. Bloomington: Indiana University Press, 1972.

Poovey, Mary. *Uneven Developments: The Ideological Work of Gender in Mid-Victorian England*. Chicago: University of Chicago Press, 1988.

Ramusack, Barbara N. "Cultural Missionaries, Maternal Imperialists, Feminist Allies: British Women Activists in India, 1865–1945." *Women's Studies International Forum* 13 (1990): 309–21.

Rendall, Jane. "'A Moral Engine'? Feminism, Liberalism, and the *English Woman's Journal*." In *Equal or Different? Women's Politics, 1800–1914*, edited by Jane Rendall, pp. 132–33. New York: Basil Blackwell, 1987.

Rendall, Jane, ed. *Equal or Different?: Women's Politics, 1800–1914*. New York: Basil Blackwell, 1987.

Rich, Adrienne. "Jane Eyre: The Temptations of a Motherless Woman." In *On Lies, Secrets, and Silence: Selected Prose, 1966–1978*, pp. 89–106. New York: W. W. Norton, 1979.

Rogers, Annie M. A. H. *Degrees by Degrees*. London, 1938.

Rose, Phyllis. *Parallel Lives: Five Victorian Marriages*. New York: Vintage Books, 1984.

Russett, Cynthia Eagle. *Sexual Science: The Victorian Construction of Womanhood*. Cambridge: Harvard University Press, 1989.

Said, Edward W. "Orientalism Reconsidered." *Cultural Critique* 6 (fall 1985): 89–107.

Sedgwick, Eve Kosofsky. *Between Men: English Literature and Male Homosocial Desire*. New York: Columbia University Press, 1985.

Showalter, Elaine. *A Literature of Their Own: British Women Novelists from Brontë to Lessing*. Princeton: Princeton University Press, 1976.

———. "The Greening of Sister George." *Nineteenth-Century Fiction* 35 (1980): 292–311.

———. *The Female Malady: Women, Madness, and Culture in England, 1830–1980*. New York: Pantheon Books, 1986.

Spivak, Gayatri Chakravorty. "Three Women's Texts and a Critique of Imperialism." *Critical Inquiry* 12, no. 1 (autumn 1985): 243–61.

Stark, Freya. Introduction to *Siamese Harem Life,* by Anna Harriette Leonowens. New York: Dutton, 1953.

Staten, Henry. "Is *Middlemarch* Ahistorical?" *PMLA* 115, no.5 (October 2000): 991–1006.

Stephen, Barbara. *Emily Davies and Girton College.* London: Constable and Co., 1927.

Strachey, Ray. *The Cause: A Short History of the Women's Movement in Great Britain.* London: G. Bell and Sons, 1928.

Sutherland, Gillian. "Education." In *The Cambridge Social History of Britain, 1750–1950,* edited by F. M. L. Thompson. Vol. 3, *Social Agencies and Institutions.* New York: Cambridge University Press, 1990.

Vicinus, Martha. *Independent Women: Work and Community for Single Women, 1850–1920.* Chicago: University of Chicago Press, 1985.

———, ed. *Suffer and Be Still: Women in the Victorian Age.* Bloomington: Indiana University Press, 1972.

Weinstein, Philip M. *The Semantics of Desire: Changing Models of Identity from Dickens to Joyce.* Princeton: Princeton University Press, 1984.

Welsh, Alexander. *George Eliot and Blackmail.* Cambridge: Harvard University Press, 1985.

Widdowson, Peter. *Hardy in History: A Study in Literary Sociology.* London: Routledge, 1989.

Yeazell, Ruth Bernard. *Fictions of Modesty: Women and Courtship in the English Novel.* Chicago: University of Chicago Press, 1991.

Zlotnick, Susan. "Jane Eyre, Anna Leonowens, and the White Woman's Burden: Governesses, Missionaries, and Maternal Imperialists in Mid-Victorian Britain." *Victorians Institute Journal* 24 (1996): 27–56.

Zonana, Joyce. "The Sultan and the Slave: Feminist Orientalism and the Structures of *Jane Eyre.*" *Signs* 18, no. 3 (spring 1993): 592–617.

Index

and gender equality, 16–17, 19
and George Eliot, 73–74, 136–37 n. 5
and liberal individualism, 99
opinion of Emily Shirreff, 15
on reading, 95
rhetorical style of, 1–4, 18–23
and students, 6, 8
Works: "Family Chronicle," 20–21;
   The Higher Education of Women, 3,
   17, 18–19, 20, 84, 95, 103; "Home
   and the Higher Education," 17;
   "Some Account of a Proposed College for Women," 93; "Special Systems of Education for Women," 17
domestic angel, 75, 102, 105
domestic ideal. *See* domestic ideology
domestic ideology, x, 6, 19–20, 25, 99
in "Of Queens' Gardens," 75–76
in *Intellectual Education and Its Influence on the Character and Happiness
   of Women,* 12–14
Dow, Leslie Smith, 64
Dowling, Linda, 109
Dyhouse, Carol, 5, 130 n.8
Eagleton, Terry, 132 n. 10
education
in *Middlemarch,* 70–73, 78–79, 81–93,
   97, 100
as social good, viii, 72–73
See also higher education movement;
   women's education
Eliot, George, 70–100, 105, 116
attitudes of:
   toward commodification, 77–78,
      86–87
   conservatism, 72
   toward higher education move-
      ment, 73–75
   toward liberal individualism, 73
   nostalgia, 86
   skepticism about educational insti-
      tutions, 72–73, 93, 99–199
   about women's sphere, 76
considered immoral, 74–75
contributions to higher education
   movement of, 71–72
death of, 101
on education as commodified, 77–78,
   86–87
and Emily Davies, 73–74, 137 n. 6
on renunciation, 77, 88–89, 99
review of *Modern Painters* by, 80–81
and Ruskin, 76–77, 80, 110

Works: *Middlemarch,* 70–72, 77–100;
   The Mill on the Floss, 78, 120, 137
   n. 9, 138 n. 15; *Selected Essays,* 105
Ellis, Sarah Stickney, 6, 10, 13, 85
eloquence, in writing of John Ruskin,
   80–81
*English Governess at the Siamese Court,
   The,* 47–69
domesticity in, 58–59
fantasy of female power in, 59–60,
   68–69
harem (Nang Harm) in, 56–57, 61–68
King Mongkut in, 52, 54–56, 57, 59,
   60, 61
marriage plot in, 53–54, 56, 68
martyrdom in, 66–67
maternity in, 66
men, Siamese, in, 50
narrative style of, 52–54, 60–61
novelization of, 53
Orientalism in, 61–62, 68
religion in, 55–56
women, Siamese, in, 50–51, 62–63,
   65–68
English Woman's Journal, The, 14–15,
   71, 97
"Female Education," 6, 63, 71
feminism, Victorian, 51, 61
and domestic ideology, 6
and liberalism, 5–6
fiction. *See* novel
flowers, women as, 81–82
Gallagher, Catherine, 137 nn. 7, 13
Gaskell, Elizabeth, 26, 130 n. 3
Gilbert, Sandra M., 37, 131 n. 7
girls' education. *See* women's education
Girton College (Cambridge), 1, 7, 16,
   70
privacy of students at, 93
Gittings, Robert, 114, 139 n. 2
Glendinning, Victoria, 8
Gosse, Edmund, 119
governess(es), 11, 26–27, 63
Governesses' Benevolent Institution, 11
Greg, W. R., 124
Grimble, Ian, 51
Griswold, A. B., 51, 135 n. 16
Gubar, Susan, 37, 131 n. 7
gynecological antifeminism, 121, 122
Hardy, Barbara, 132 n. 15
Hardy, Emma Gifford, 114–15
Hardy, Florence Dugdale, 103, 114–15,
   116

and heterosexuality, 116
self-representation of, 115
Marcus, Sharon, 29
marriage plot, ix–xi, 102
  in *The English Governess at the
    Siamese Court*, 48, 53–54
  in *Jude the Obscure*, 128
Martineau, Harriet, 26, 135 n. 24
Maudsley, Henry, "Sex in Mind and
  Education," 122–23
Maurice, F. D., 24
Maynard, Constance, 7, 9, 70
metaphor(s)
  in *Middlemarch*, 80, 81–82
  in *The Mill on the Floss*, 137 n. 9
  in "Of Queens' Gardens," 81
Michie, Helena, 30
Middlemarch, 70–72, 77–100, 110
  characters in: Dorothea Brooke,
    70–71, 87–93; Mary Garth, 92–93,
    94–98; Tertius Lydgate, 80, 82–84;
    Rosamund Vincy, 80, 81–87; Will
    Ladislaw, 90–91
  composition of, 136 n. 1
  critical responses to, 91, 136 n. 3
  domestic ideology in, 80
  education in, 136 n. 2
    dilettante, 81–92; ideal function of,
    87–88; Oxbridge, critique of,
    78–79; relational model of, 92–93;
    self-, 97, 100; women's, as topic,
    70–73
  family ties in, 93–94, 100
  library in, 89–91, 94–95
  marriage in, 83–84, 85, 88
  melancholy in, 91, 98
  metaphors in, 80, 82
  nostalgia in, 86, 98–99
  reading in, 94–96
  retrospective setting of, 72
  writing in, 96–97
Mill, John Stuart, 28, 72, 125
  arguments for women's education of,
    84–85
  Charlotte Brontë's opinion of, 26
  On Liberty, 25
  "On the Subjection of Women," 20
Millgate, Michael, 139 n. 2
Mills, Sara, 48–49, 51, 52, 134 n. 11
Moglen, Helene, 132 n. 16
Mongkut, King, 52, 54–56, 57, 59, 60,
  61
Morgan, Susan, 66, 133 n. 2, 136 n. 25
Morris, Mowbray, 117

"New Woman," 102–3, 121
novel
  as feminine genre, 105
  and higher education movement,
    viii–xi
  working-class hero in, 106
"Of Queens' Gardens," 75–76, 77, 80,
  95
Pair of Blue Eyes, A, 103, 106, 107–12
  effeminacy of male characters in,
    111–13
  heterosexual relations in, 109–10, 111
  homosocial relations in, 111
  intellectual ambition in, 108–9
  mentorship, male, in, 109–10
  plot of, 107–8
Parkes, Bessie Rayner, 25
Paul, Saint, 1–2
Poovey, Mary, 105, 132 n. 20, 139 n. 4
Princess, The, 43–44
Queen's College, 11
Quiggin, M. A., 8
Ramusack, Barbara, 52
Rich, Adrienne, 132 n. 16
Rigby, Elizabeth, 26–27, 120, 131 n. 10
Romance of the Harem, The
  harem (Nang Harm) in, 65, 67–68
  narrative style of, 52
Ruskin, John, 75–76, 80–81, 94, 95
Said, Edward, 49, 51
Saturday Review, 120
Sedgwick, Eve Kosofsky, 106, 110
"Sex in Mind and Education," 122
Sheets, Robin Lauterbach, 75
Shirreff, Emily
  discussed in *English Women's Journal*,
    15
  and domestic ideology, 12–14
  *Intellectual Education, and Its Influ-
    ence on the Character and Happiness
    of Women*, 12–14
Showalter, Elaine, 136 n. 4
Sidgwick, Henry, 16–17
Spivak, Gayatri, 27–28
Staten, Henry, 138 n. 18
Sutherland, Gillian, 5
Tennyson, Alfred, Lord, 43–44
Veeder, William, 75
Vicinus, Martha, 11
Weinstein, Philip M., 139 n. 6
Welsh, Alexander, 136 n. 2
Widdowson, Peter, 104, 107
Wollstonecraft, Mary, 85, 135 n. 19
Wolstenholme, Elizabeth, 4, 137 n. 11

women, Victorian
  ambitious, 85–86
  as authors, 102, 117
  in fiction, 102–3
  metaphors about, 81–82
  pedagogic mission of, 49
  and public speaking, 2
  scientific theories about, 102, 121
  and social class, 5, 7–8, 121
  sphere of, 6, 12–13
women's education. *See also* higher education movement
  "accomplishments" in, 9, 83, 110
  goals of, 14–17
  inadequacy of, 10–11
  and maternity, 122
  nineteenth-century literature of, 9–10, 12–15, 17–20
  Ruskin, theory of, 75–76
  as theme in *Middlemarch,* 70–73
  in universities, 5
women's education movement. *See* higher education movement
Yeazell, Ruth Bernard, x
Yonge, Charlotte M., 85
Zlotnick, Susan, 133 n. 6